I love you

VALENTINE
COLORING BOOK
RELAXING DESIGNS

▲ ART THERAPY COLORING

Preview of Coloring Pages

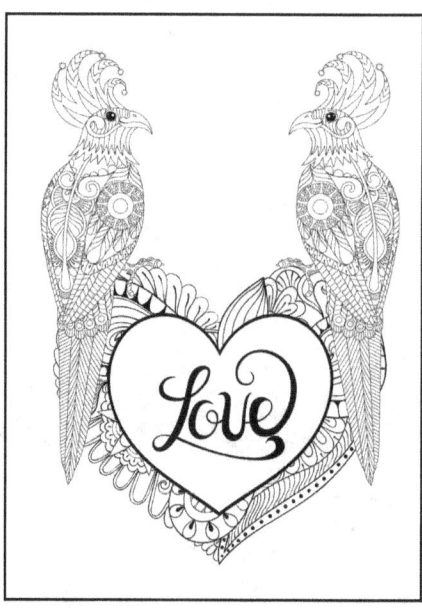

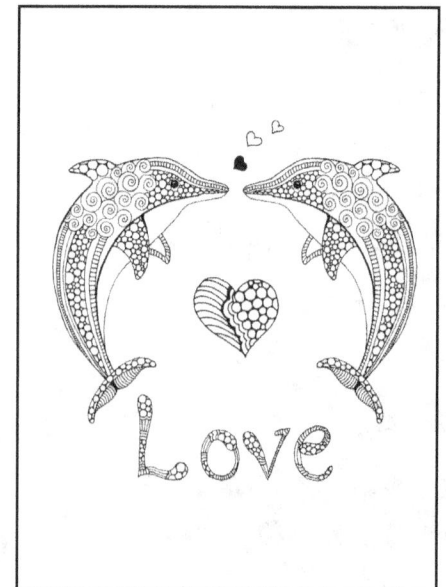

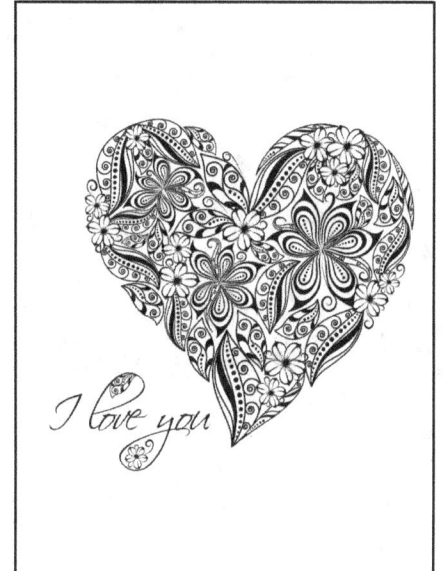

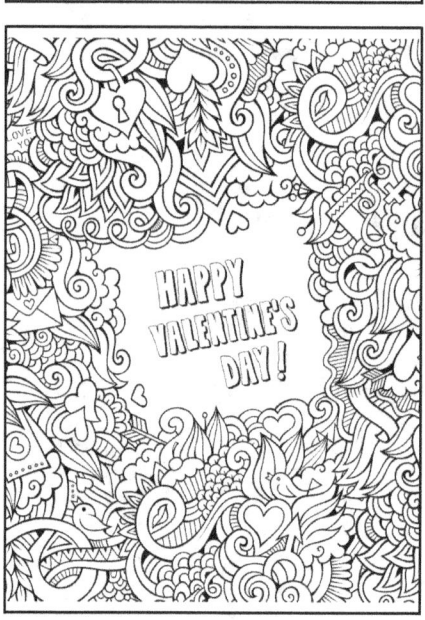

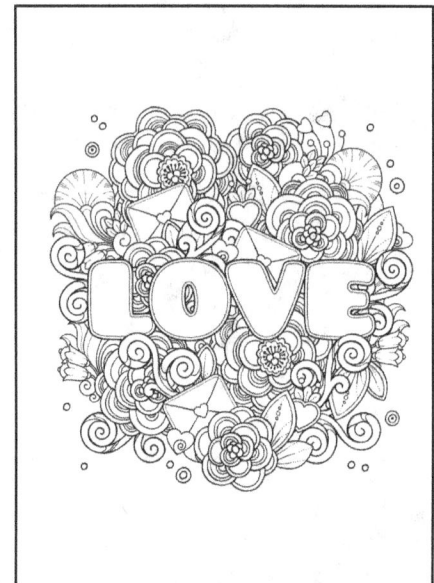

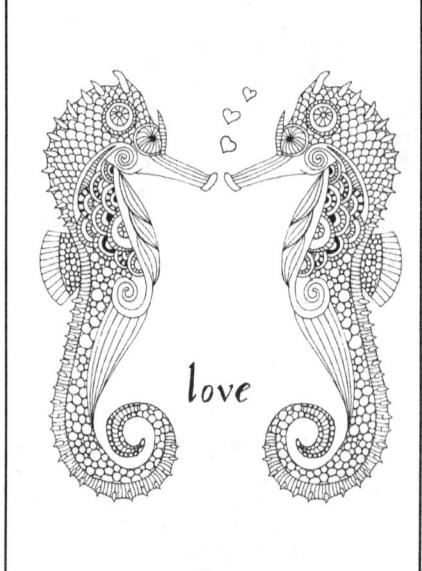

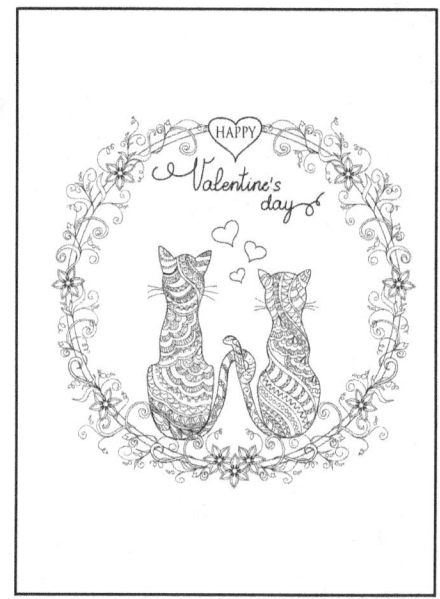

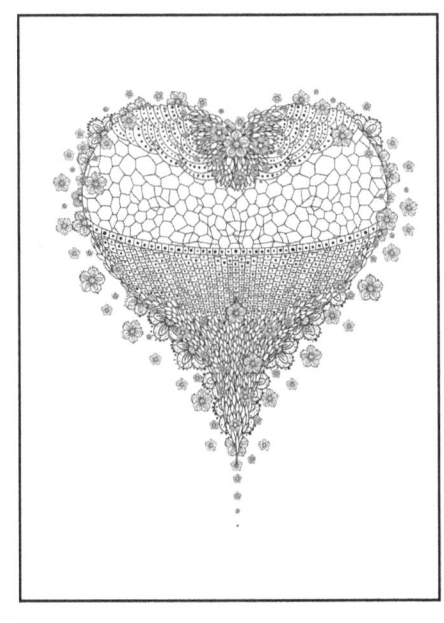
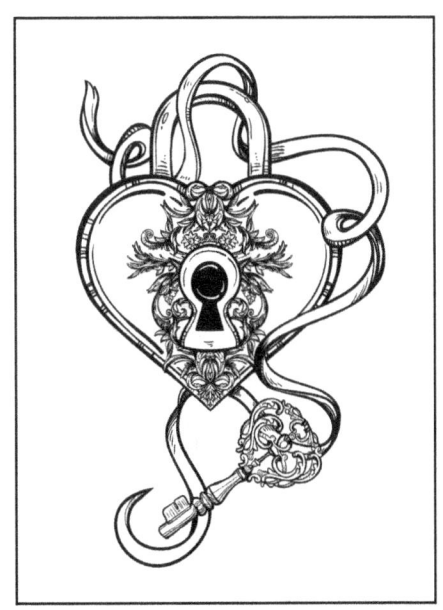
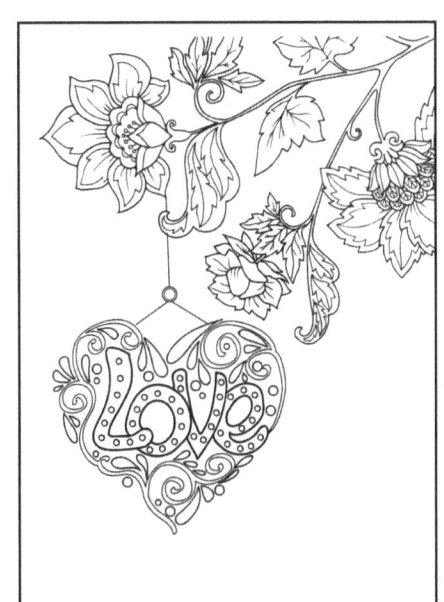
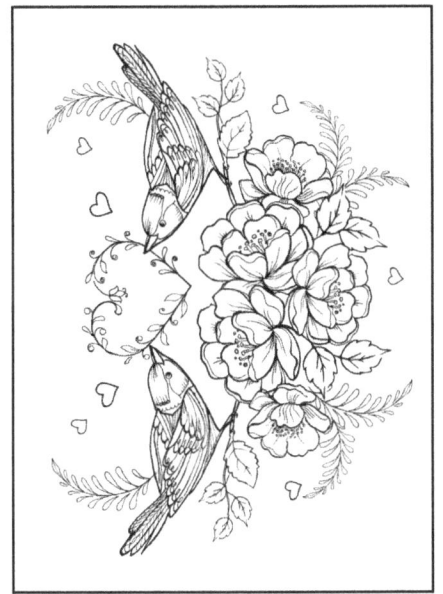
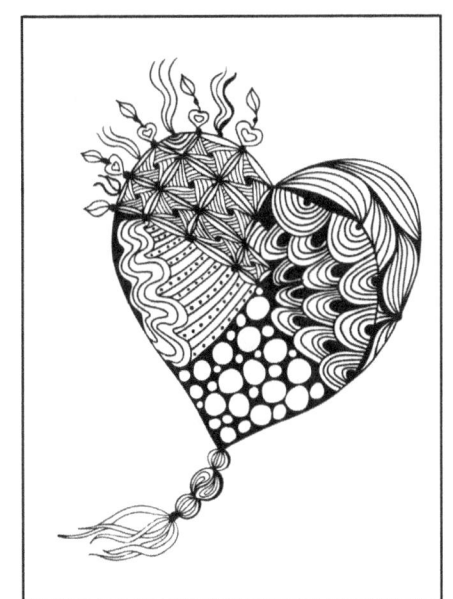
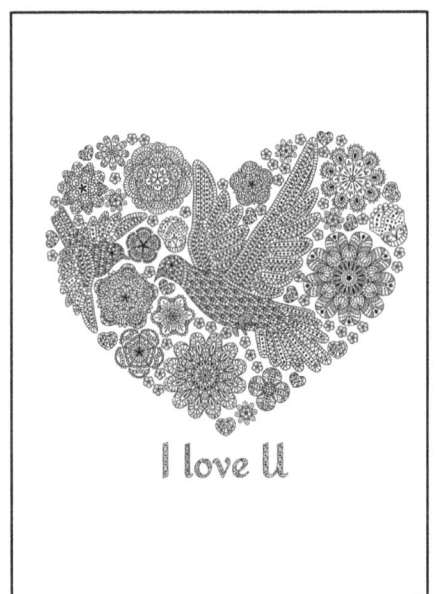
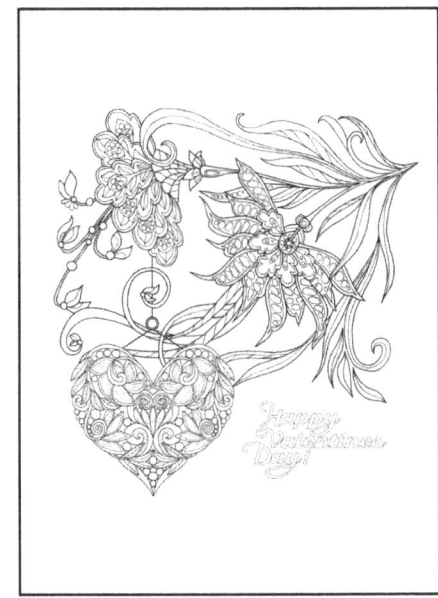
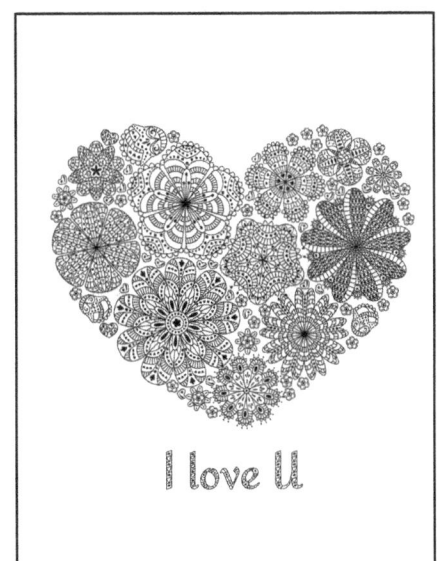
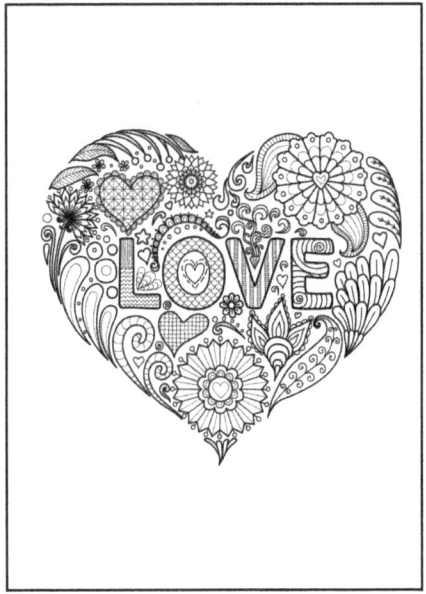

Preview of Coloring Pages

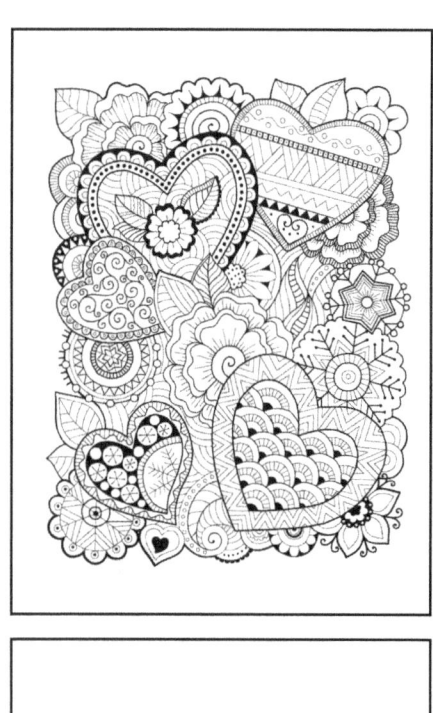
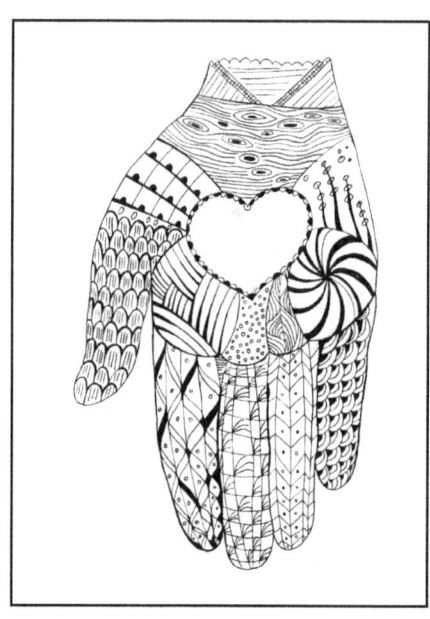
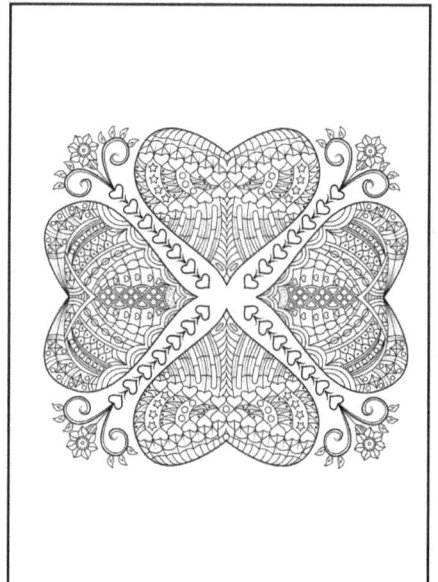
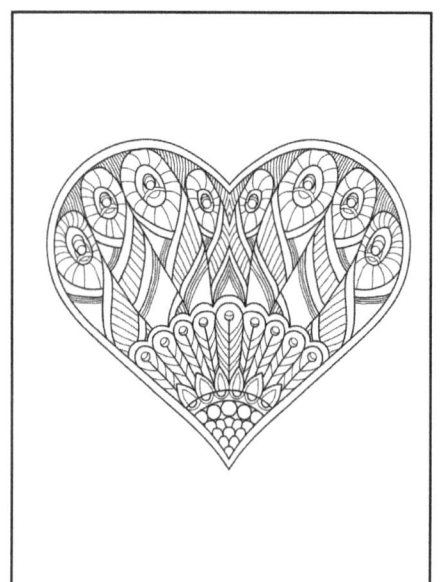
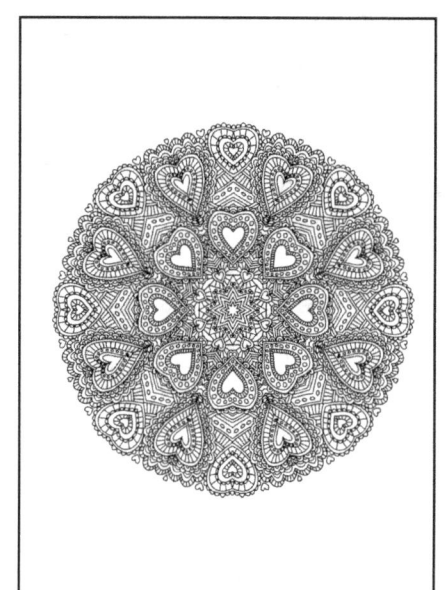
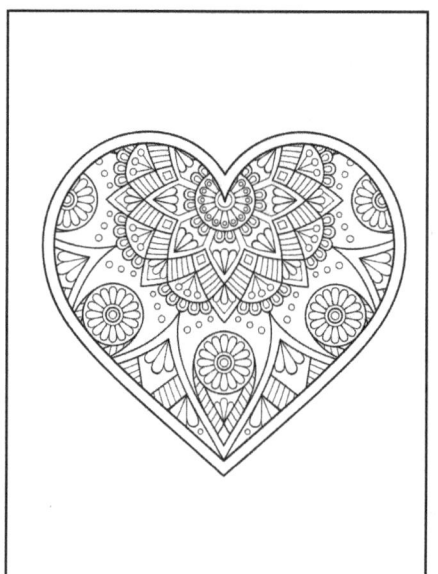
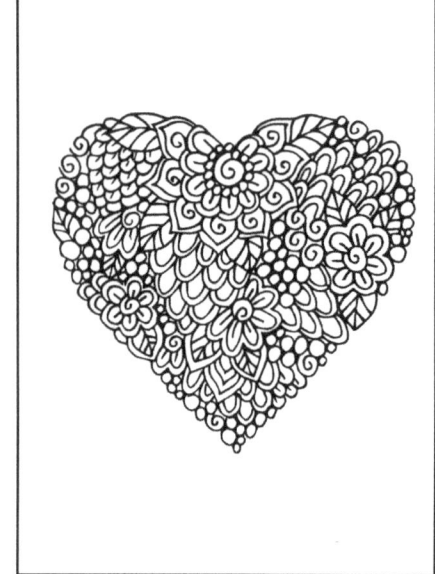
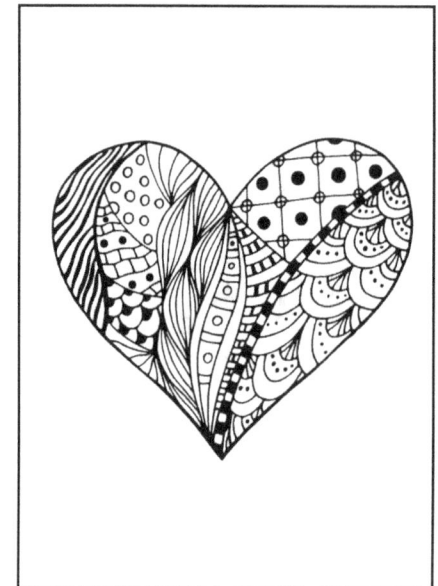
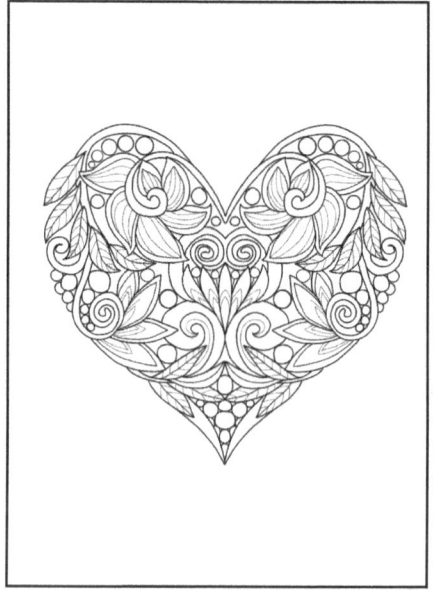

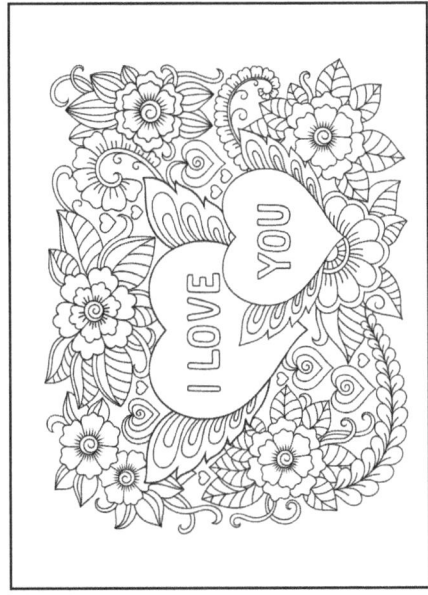

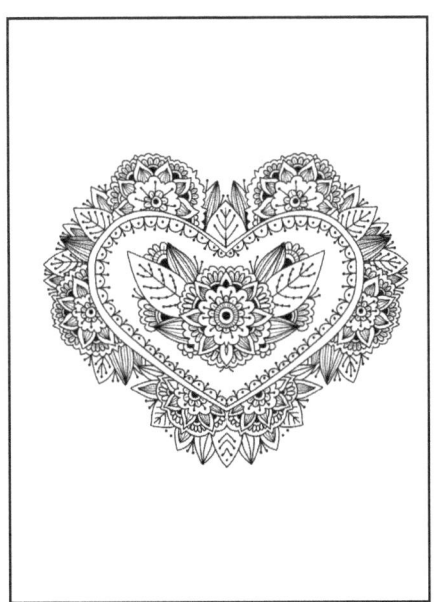

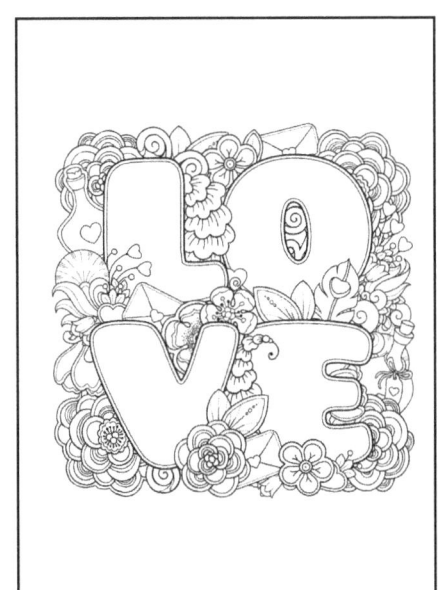

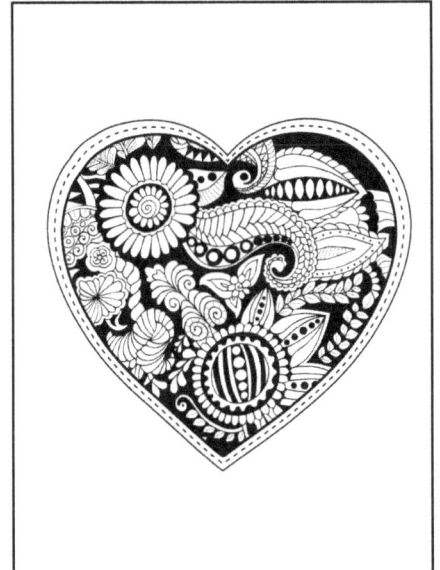

Happy Valentine's day

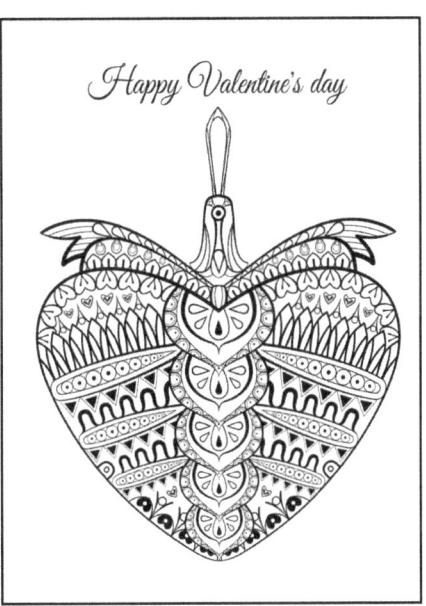

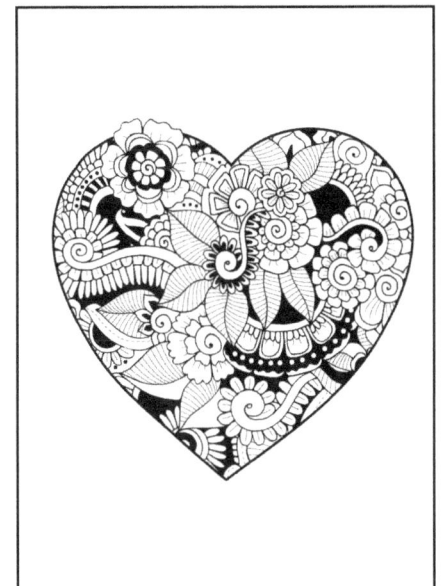

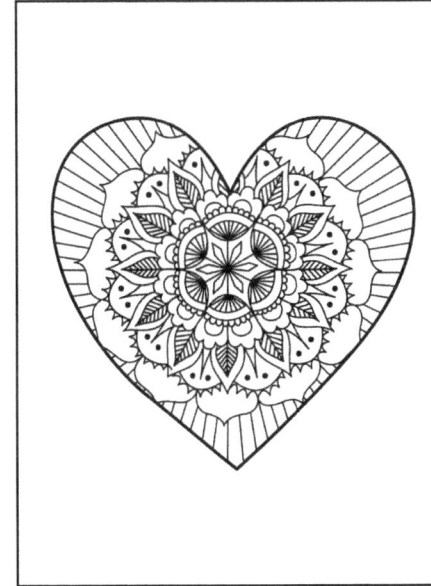

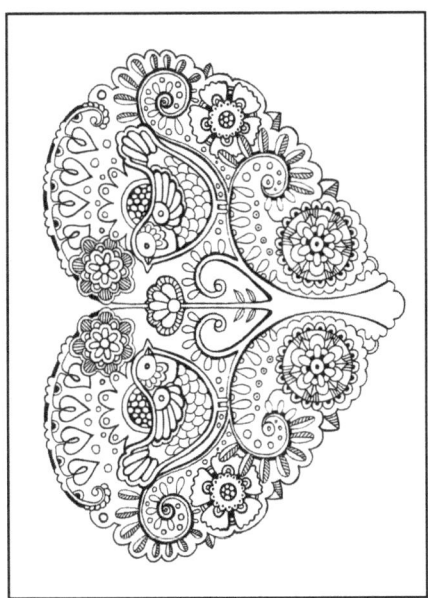

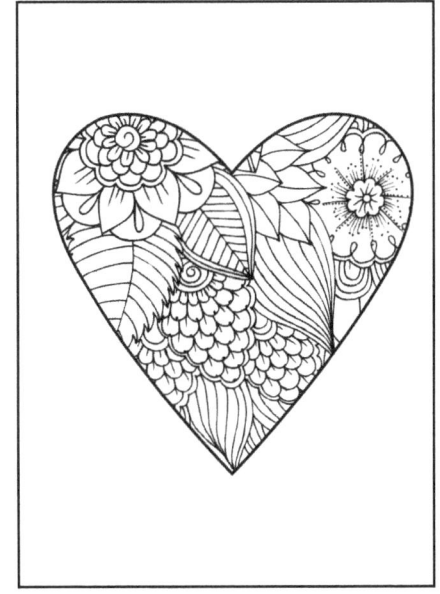

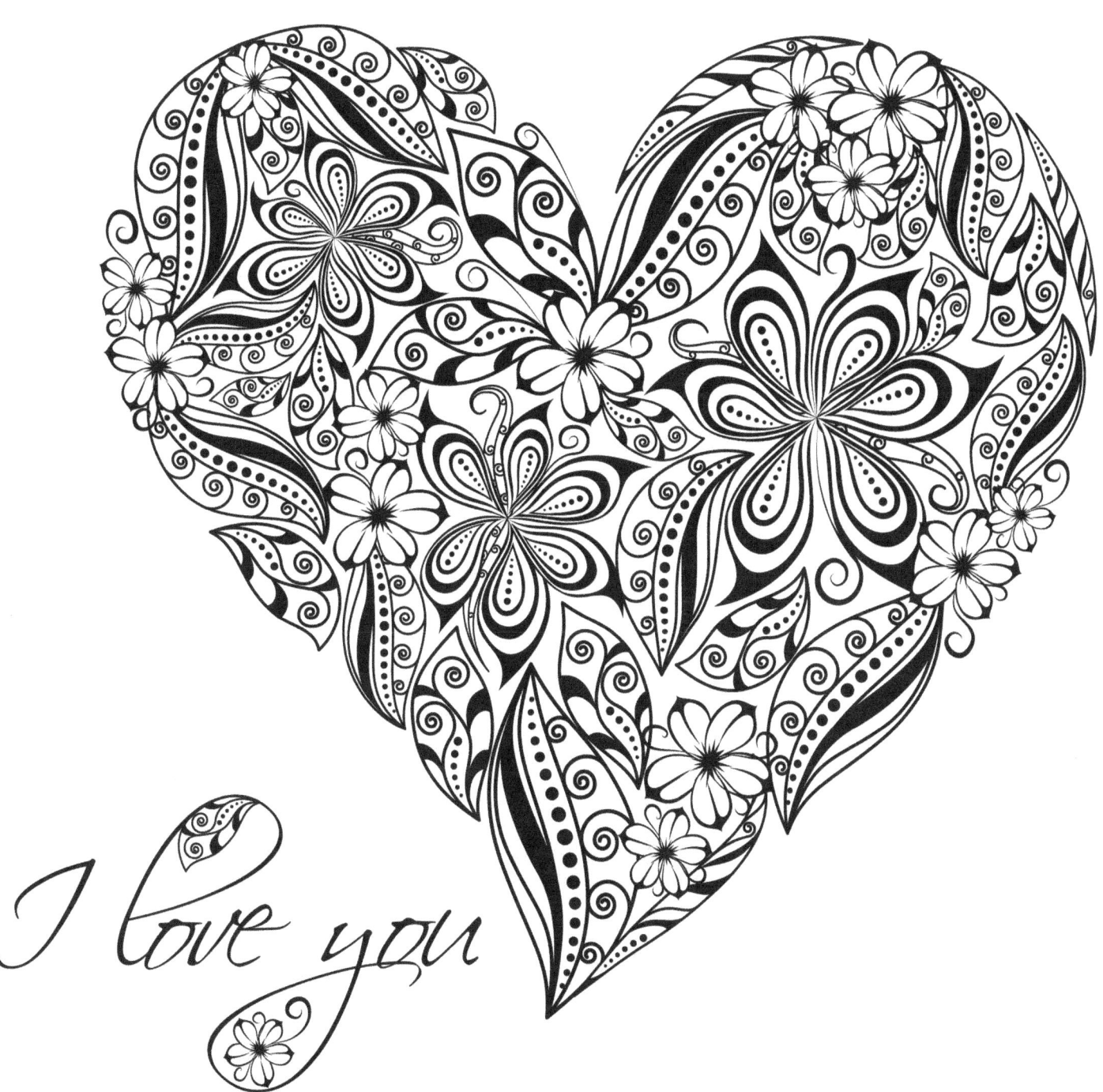

I love you

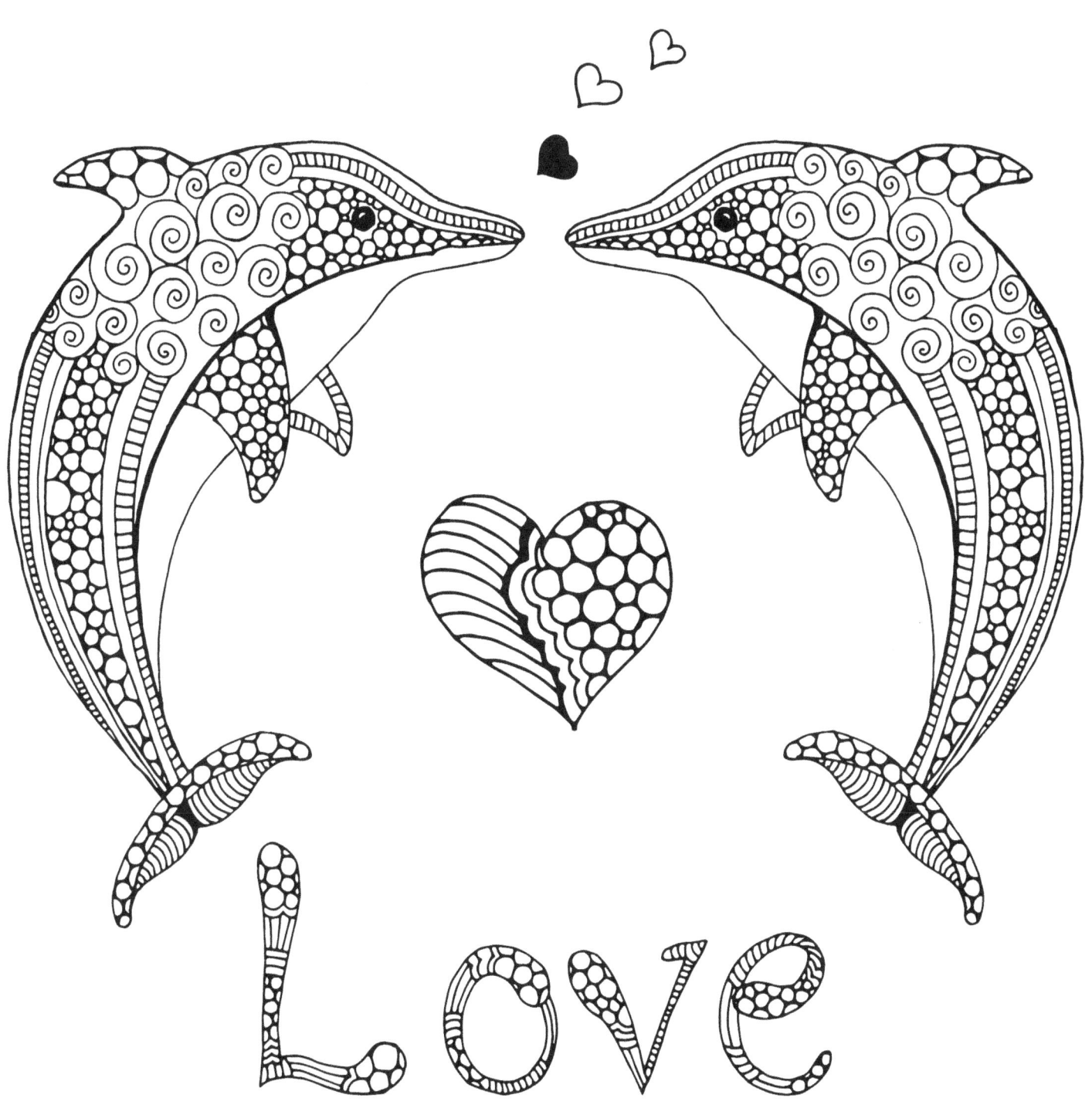

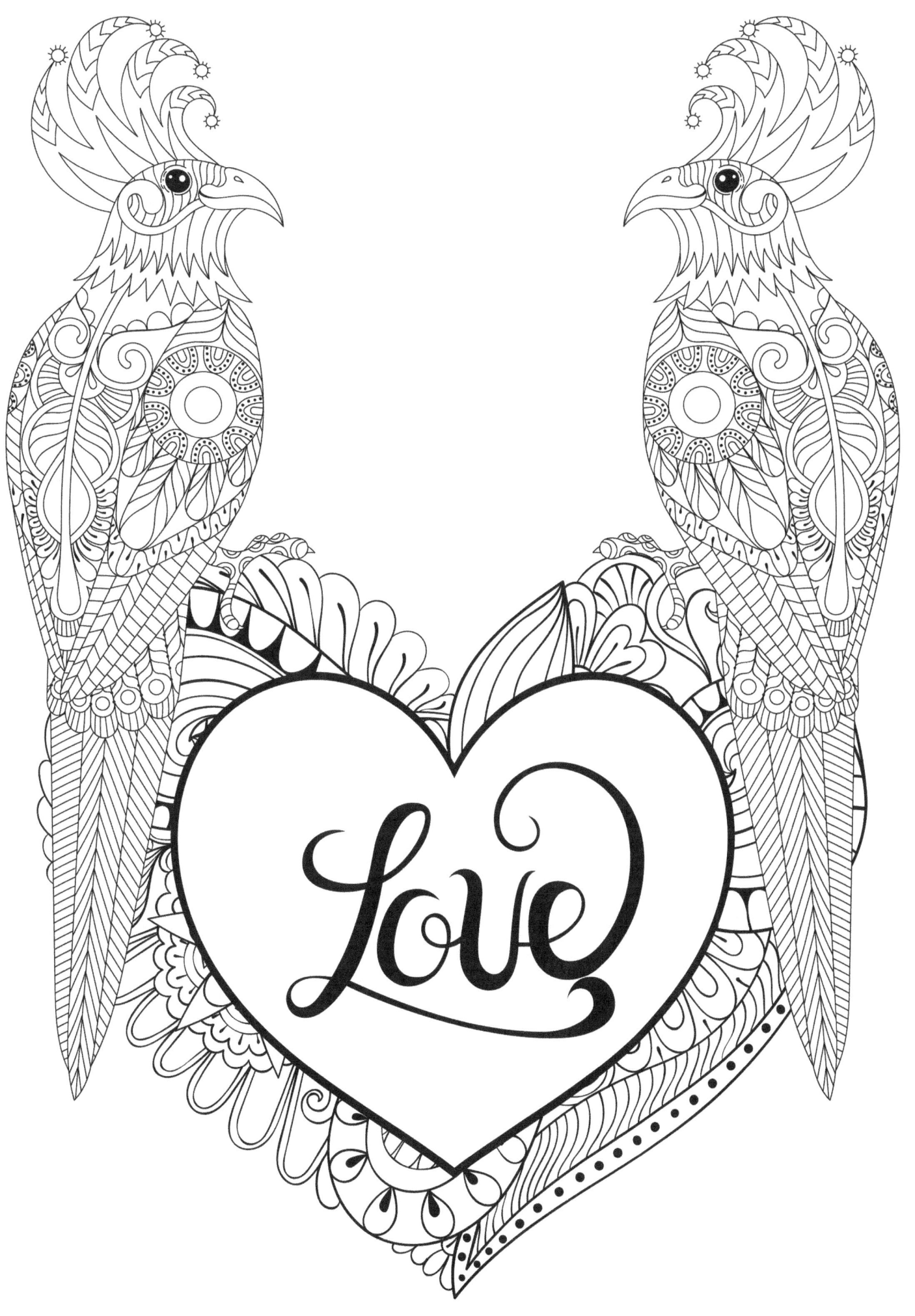

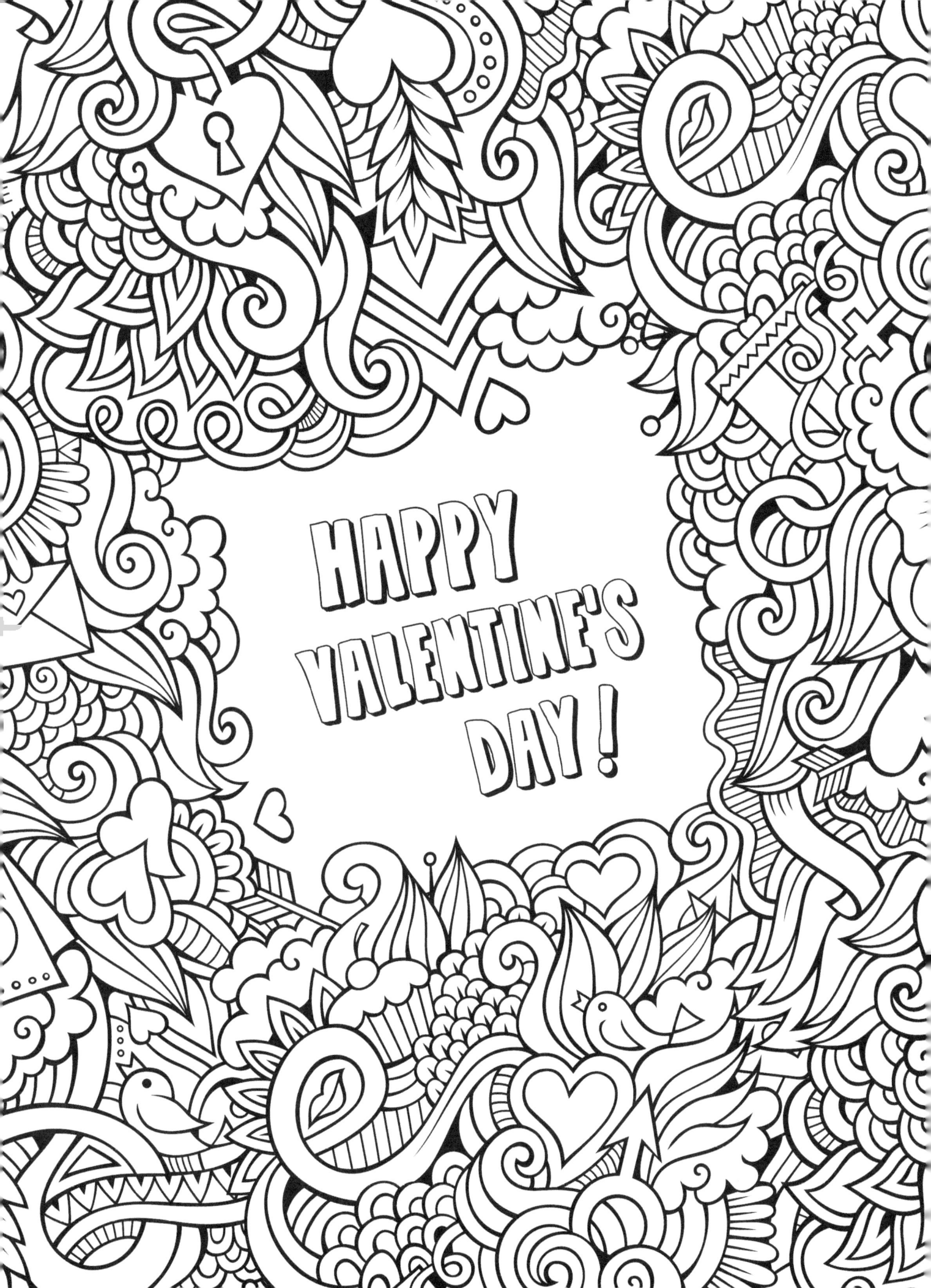

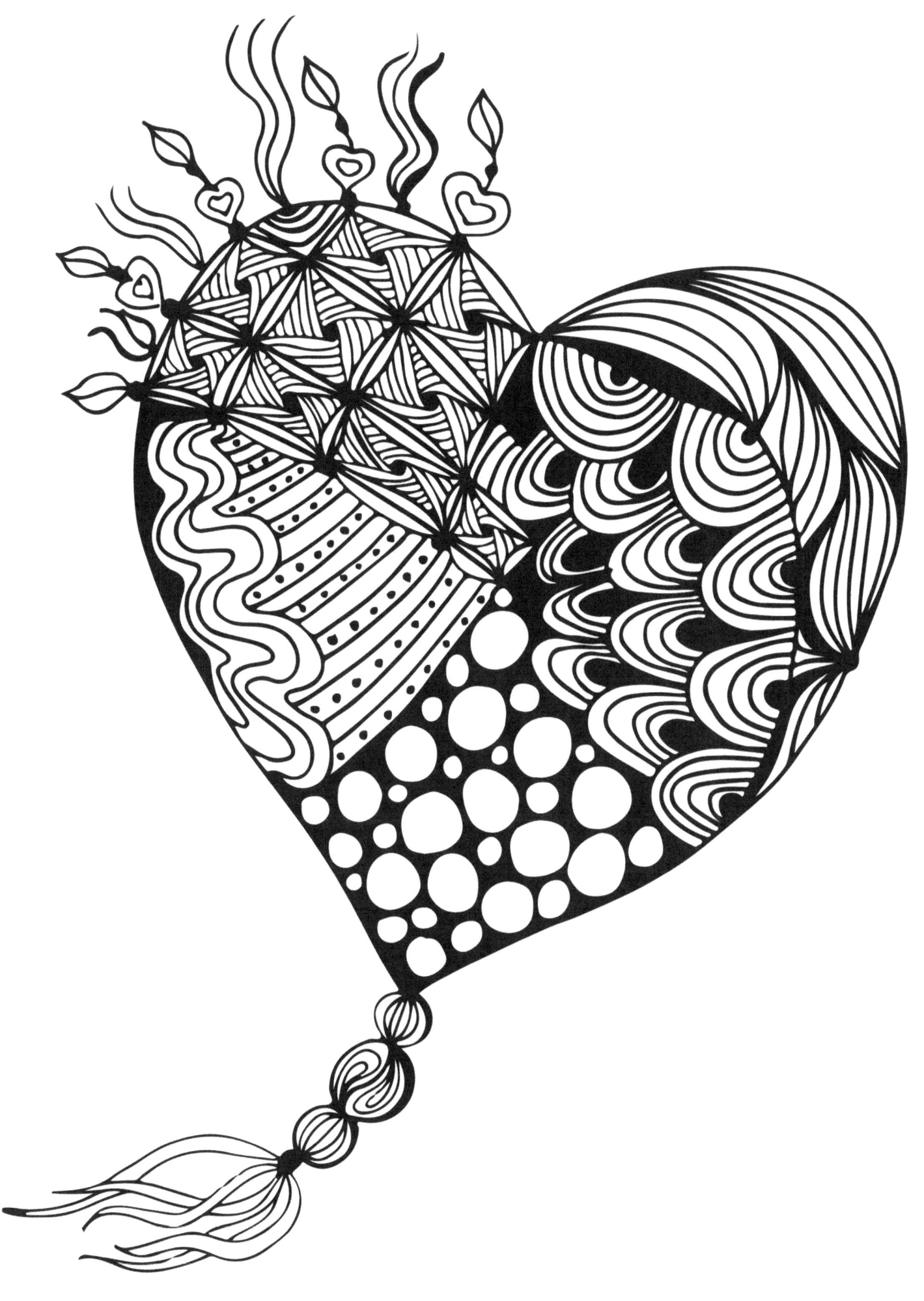

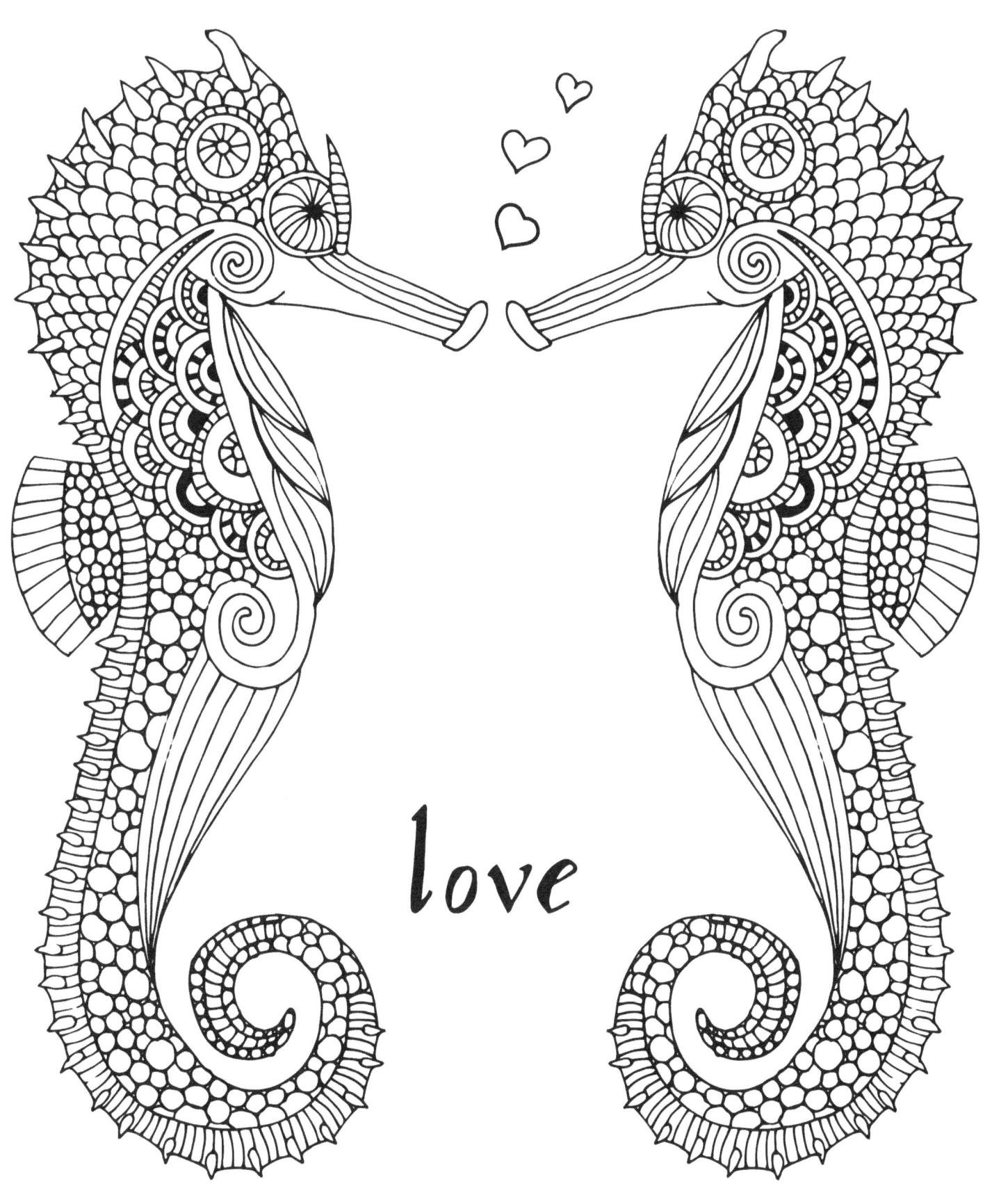

love

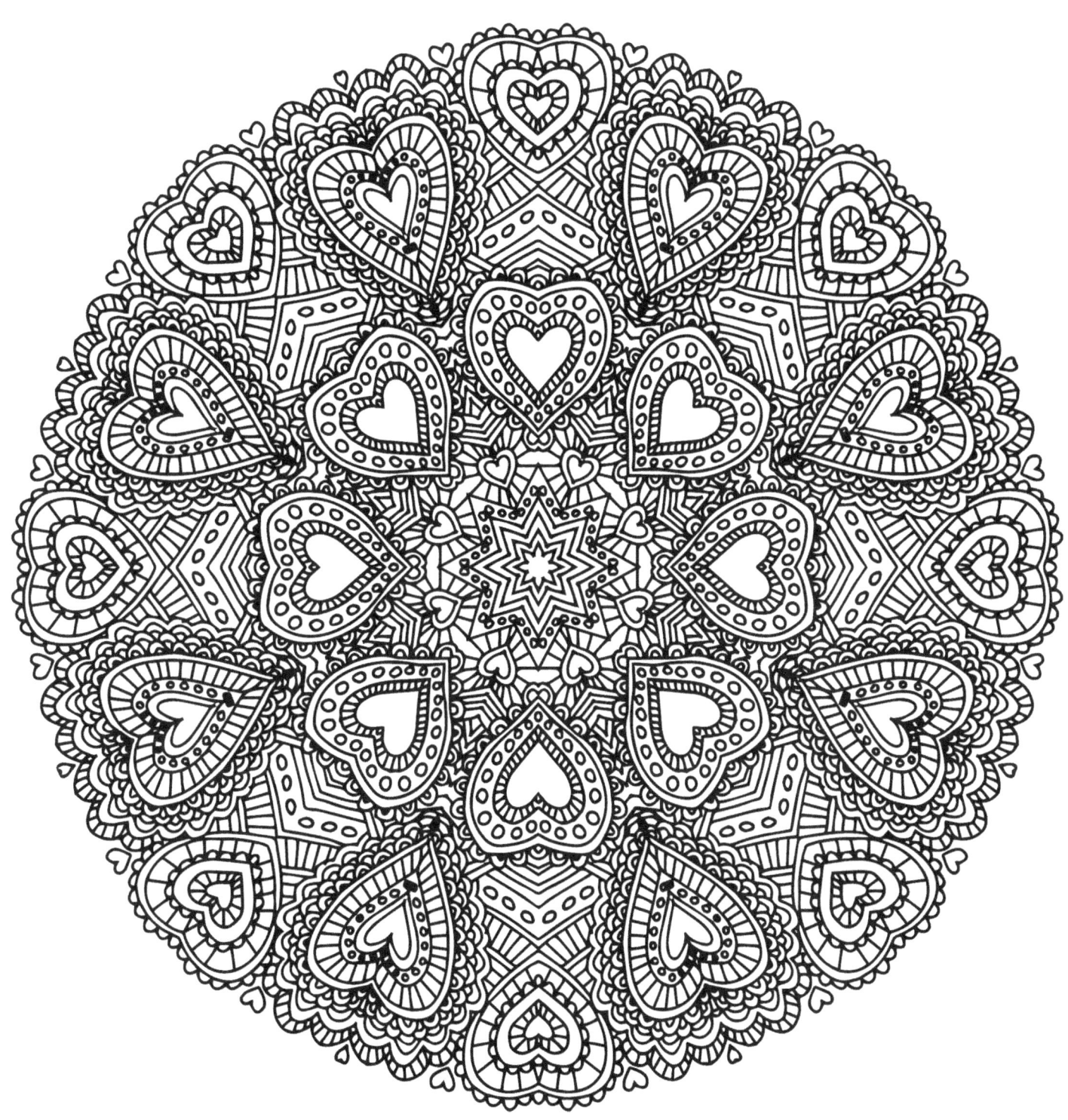

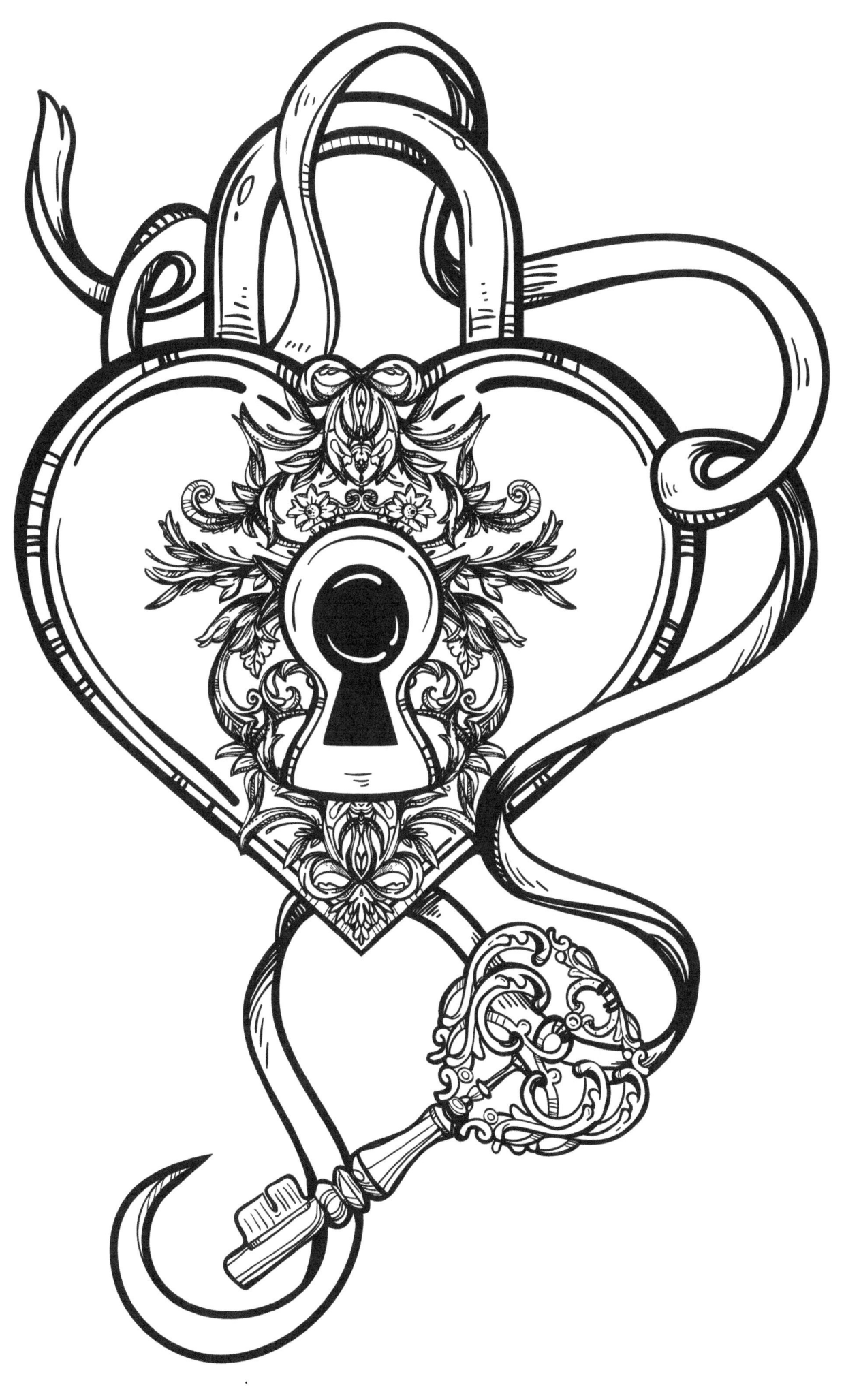

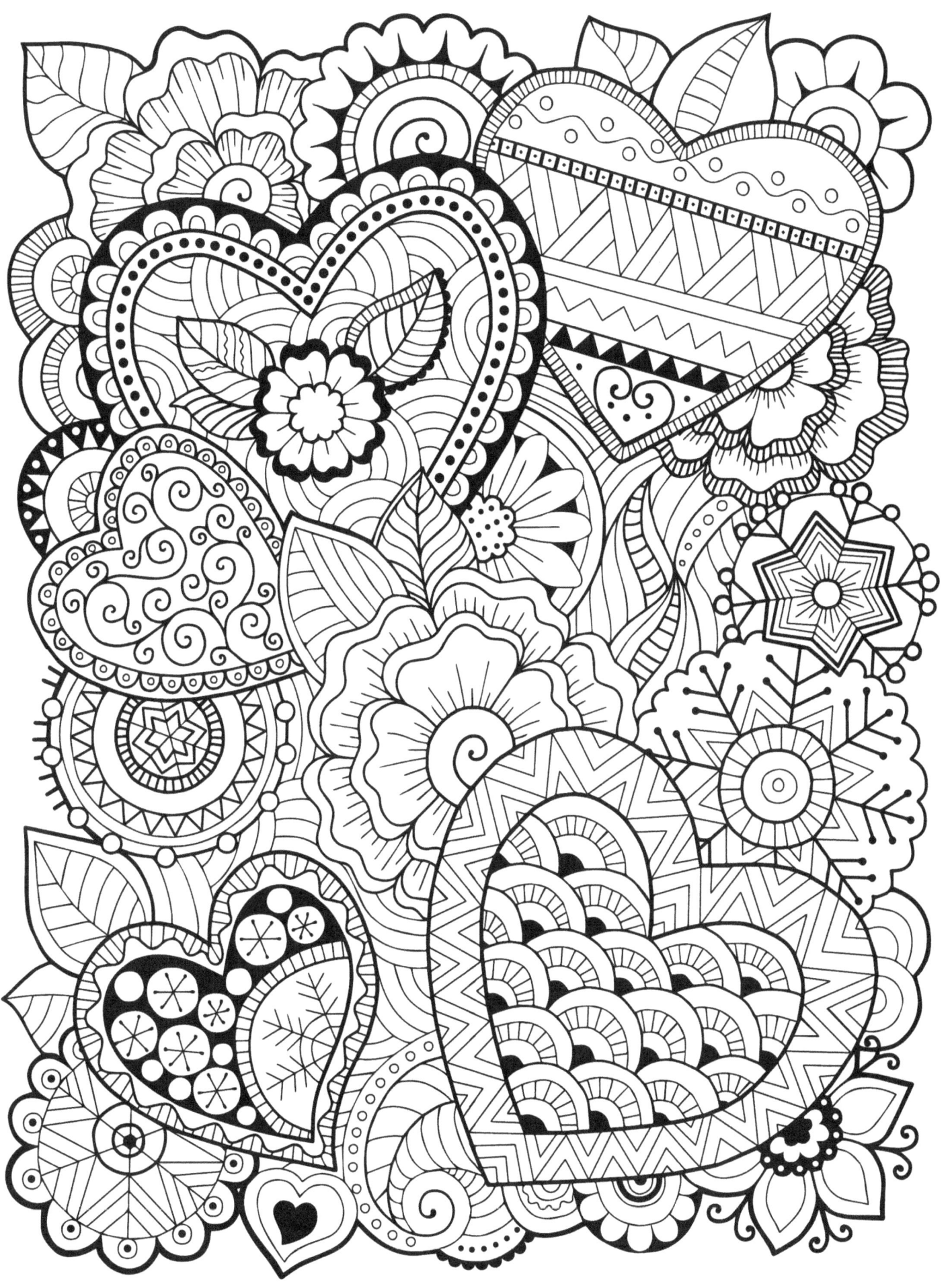

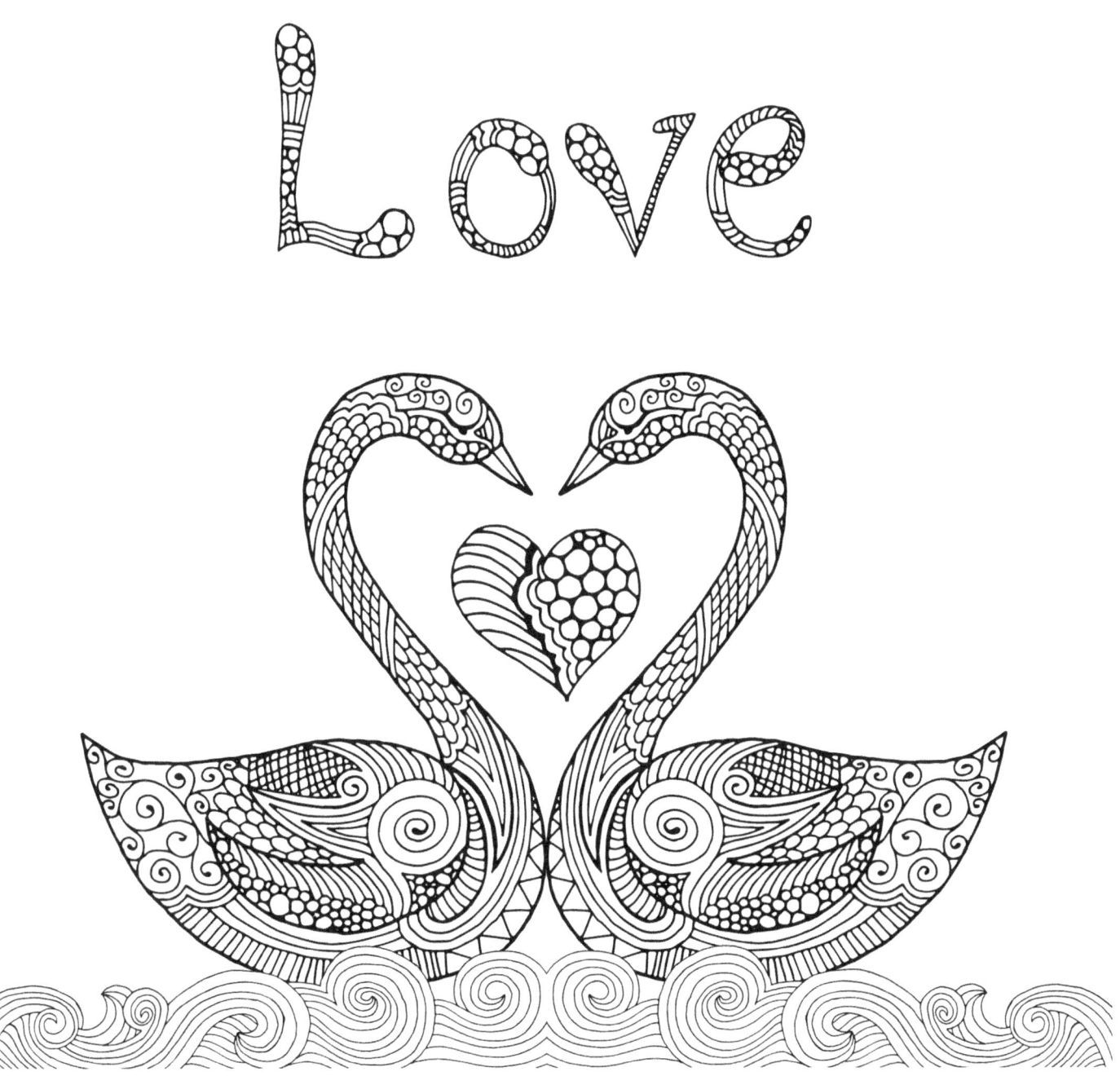

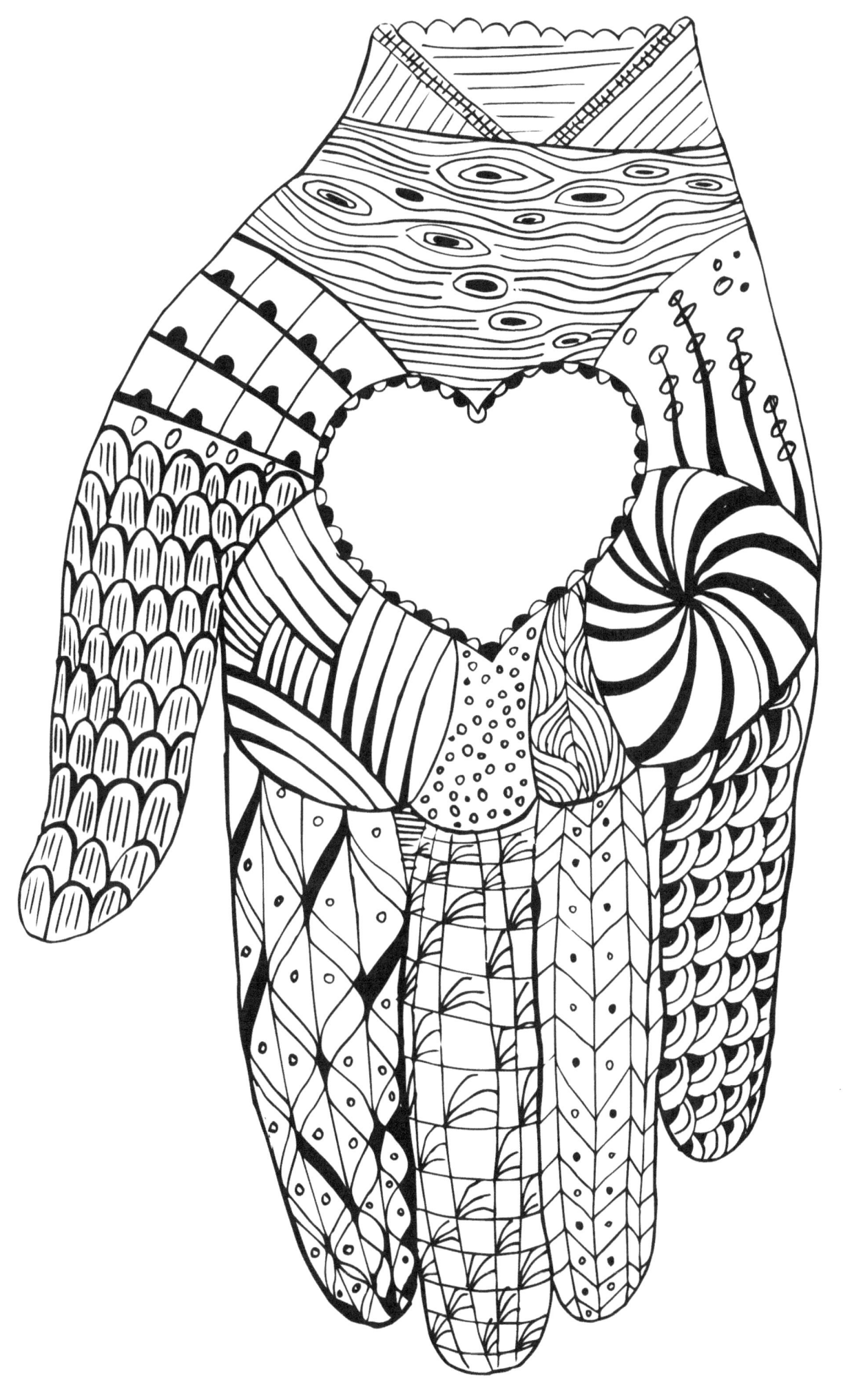

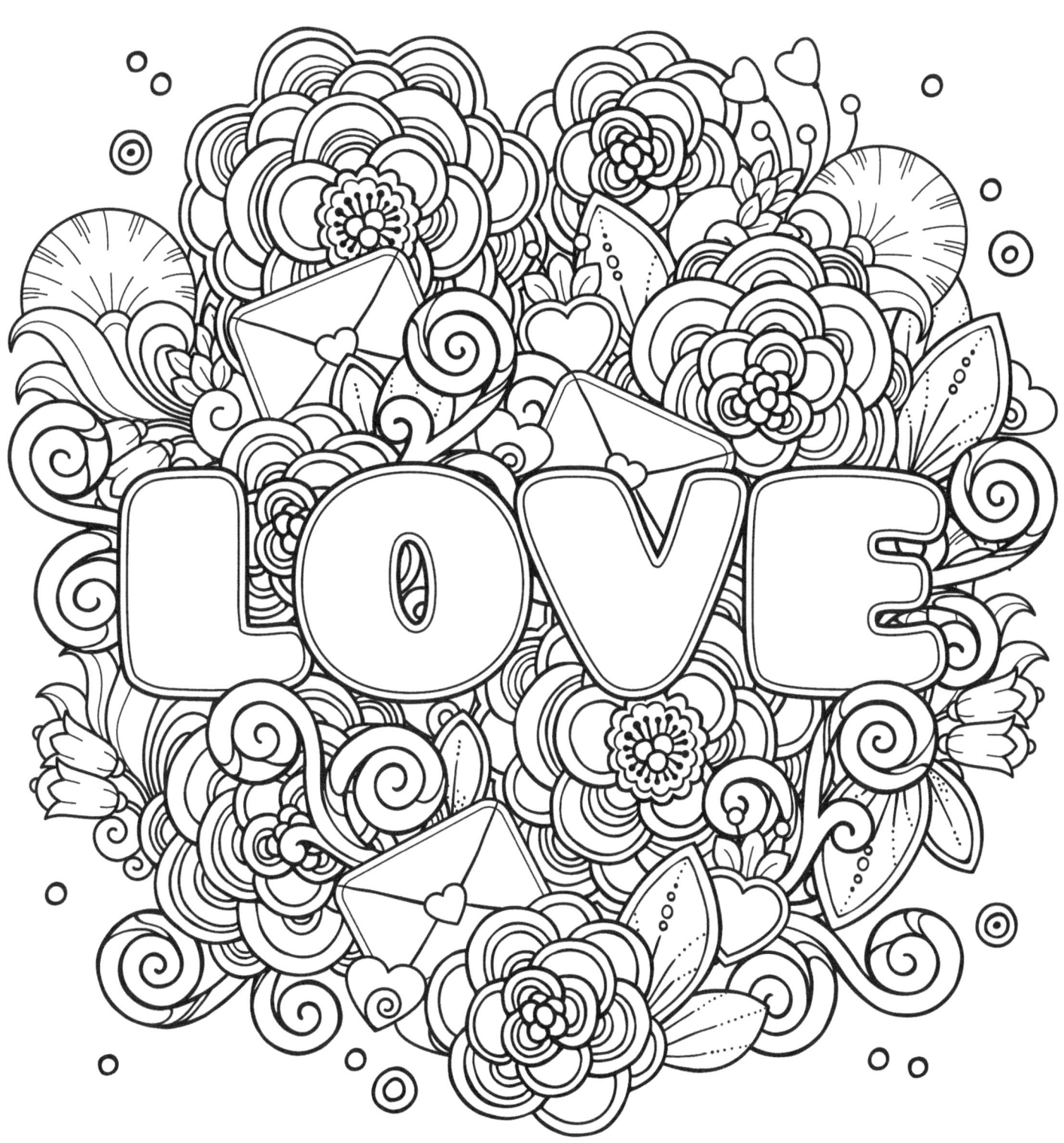

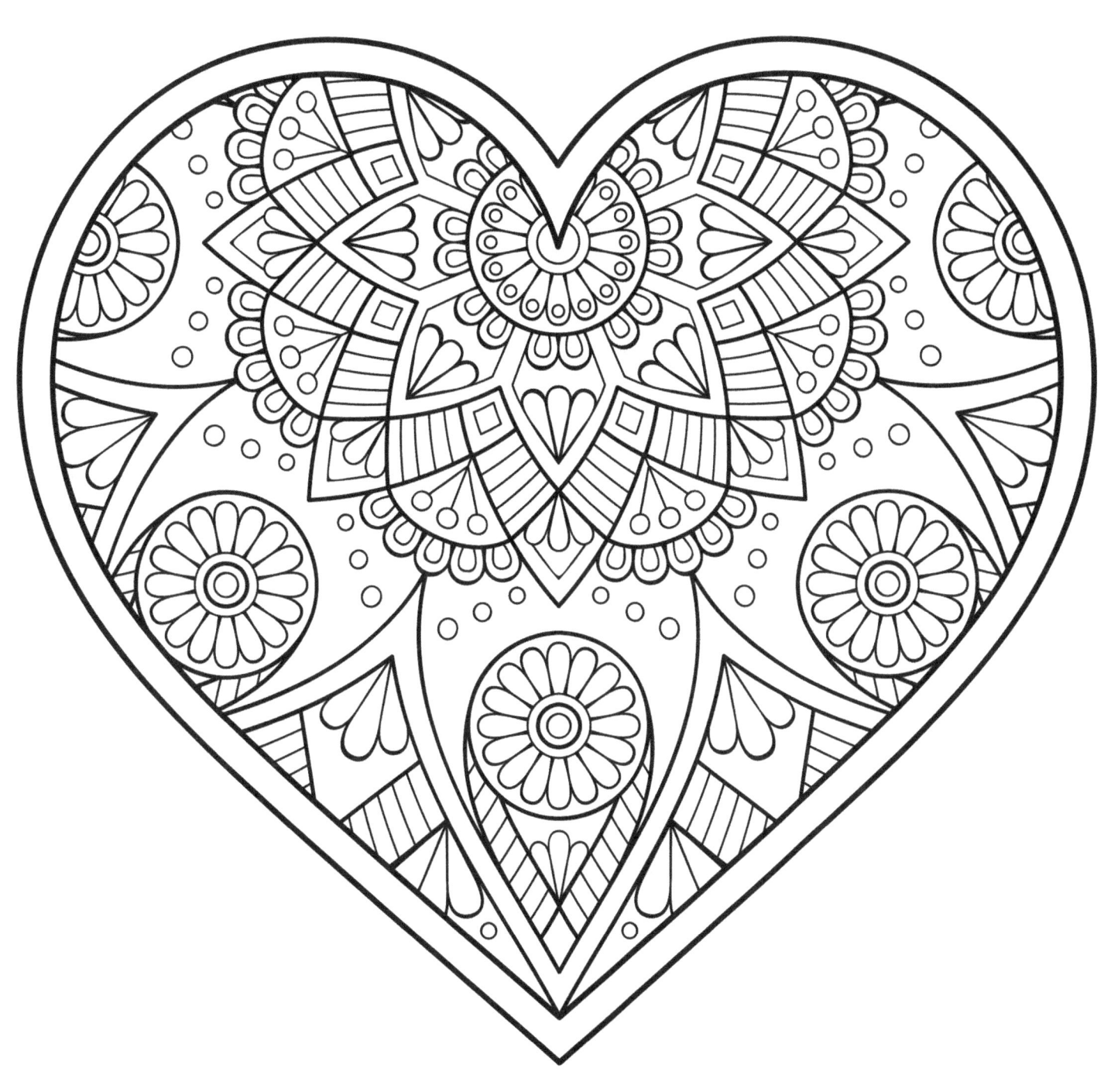

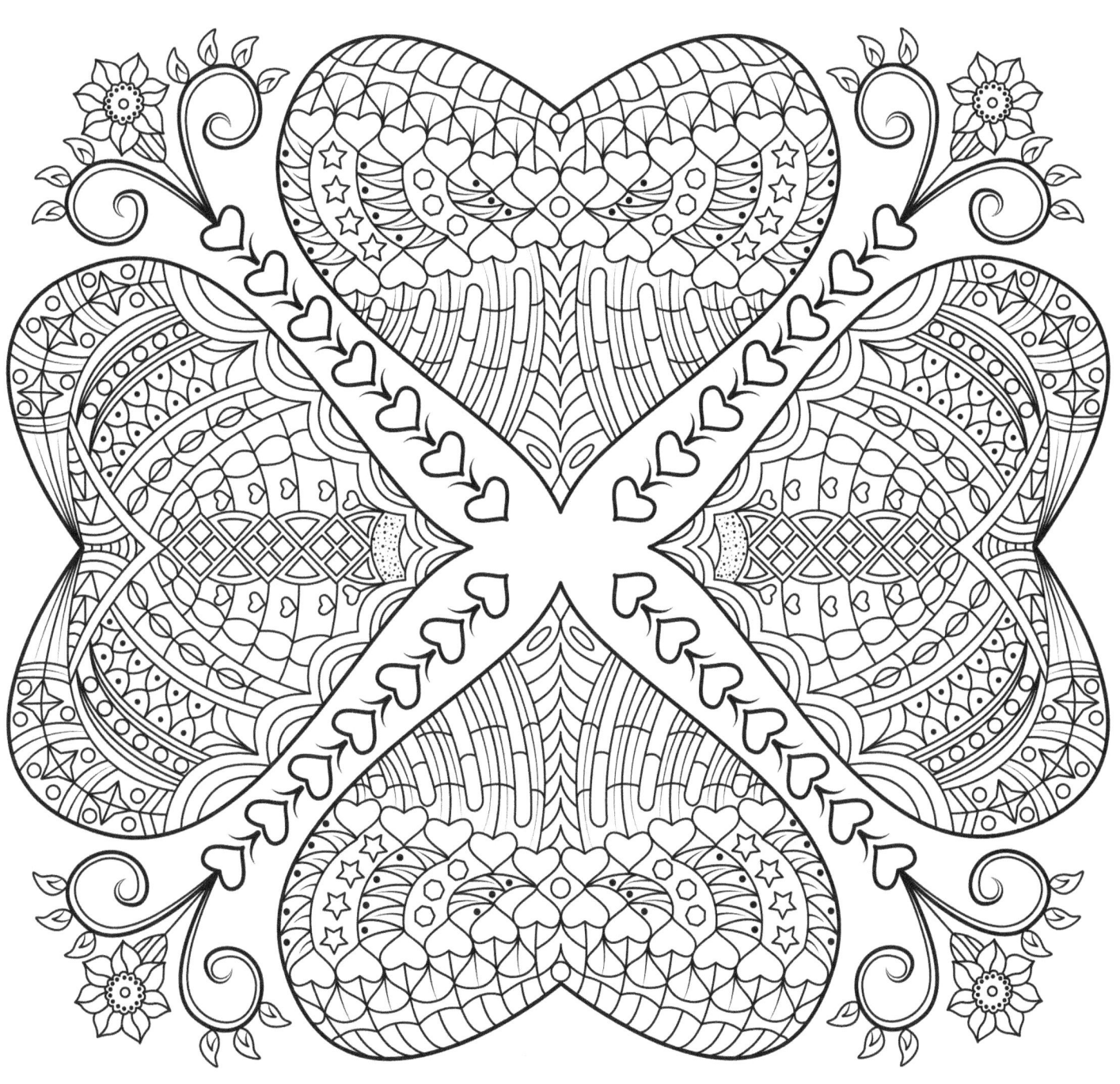

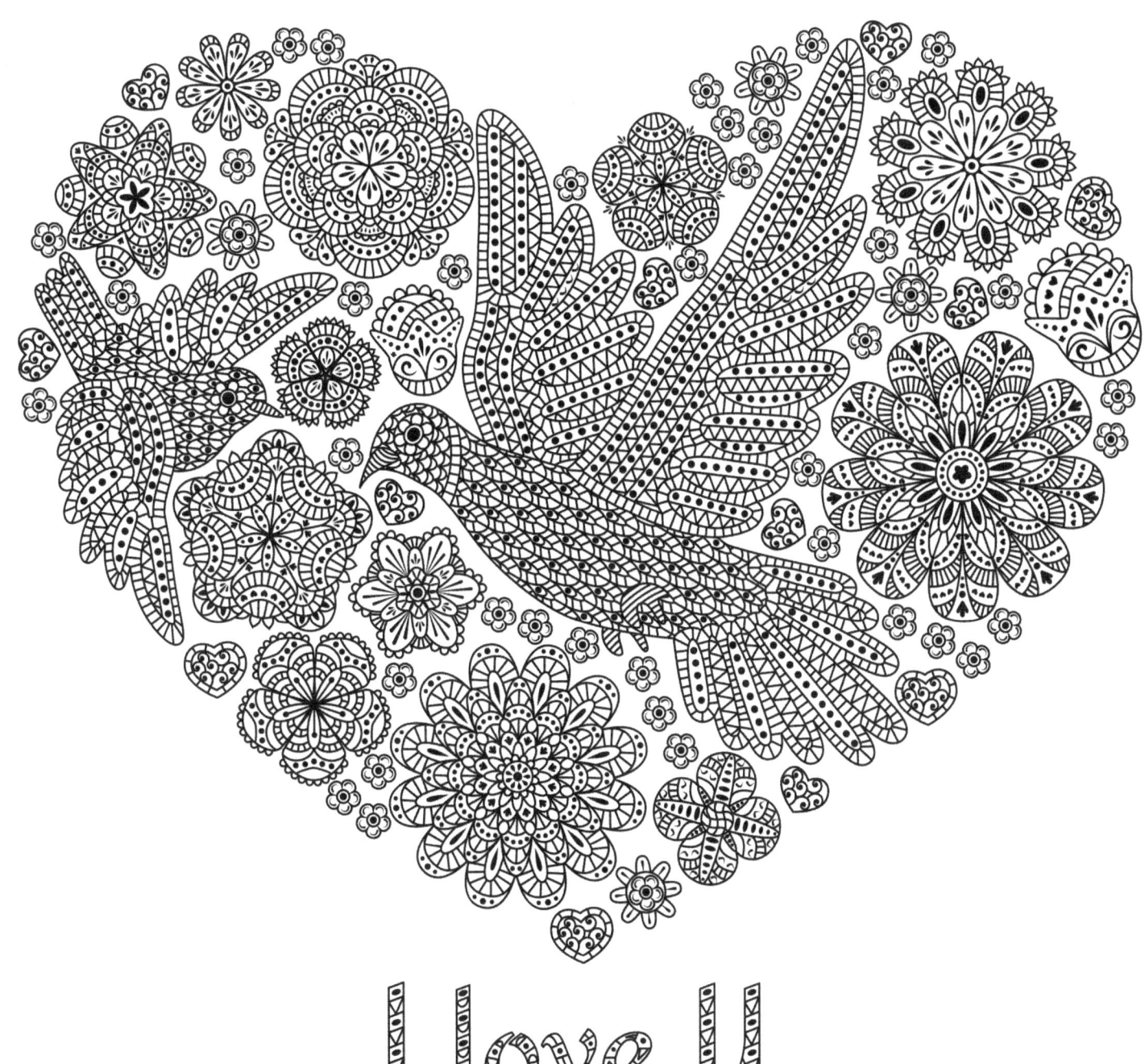

I love U

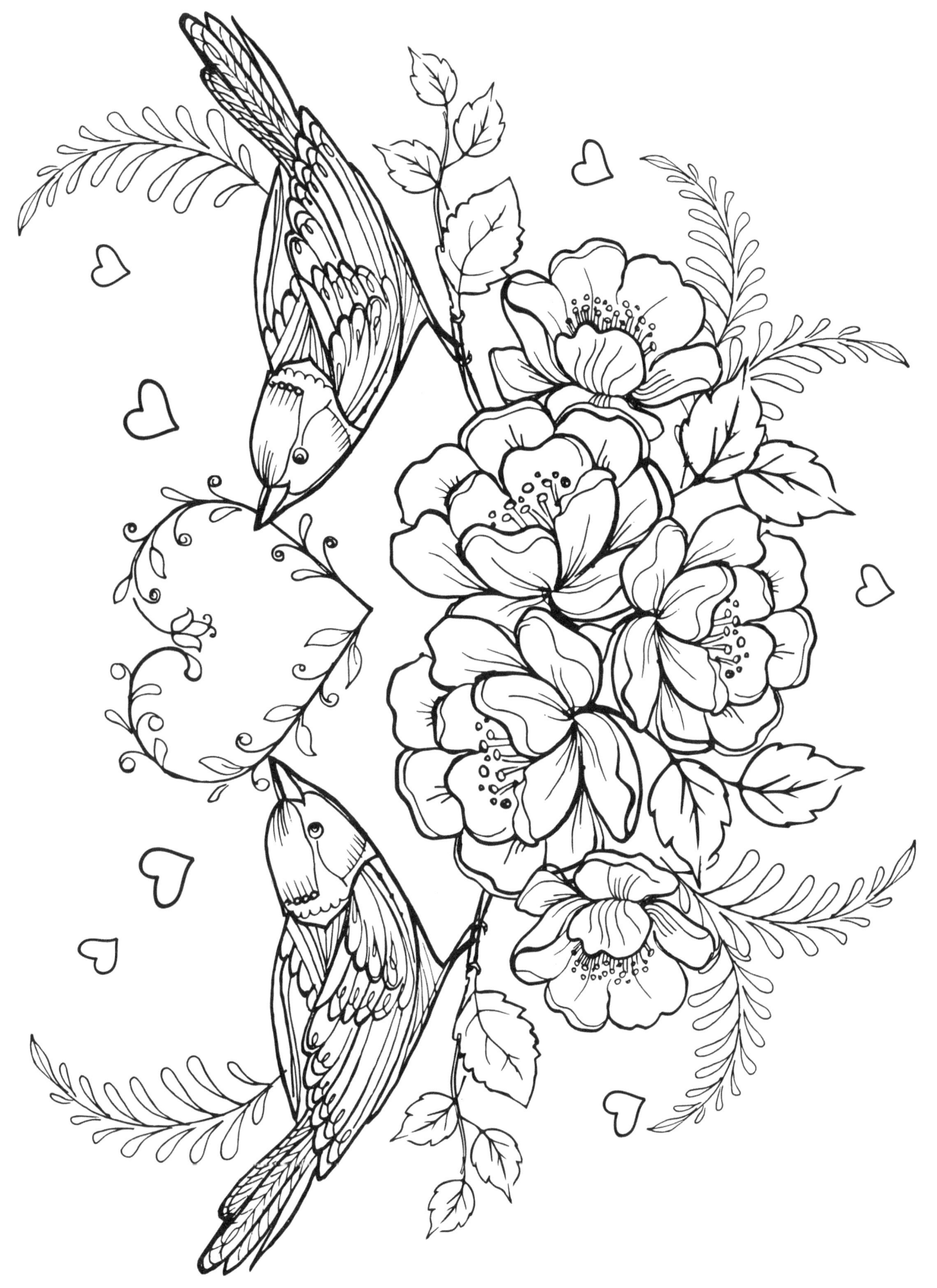

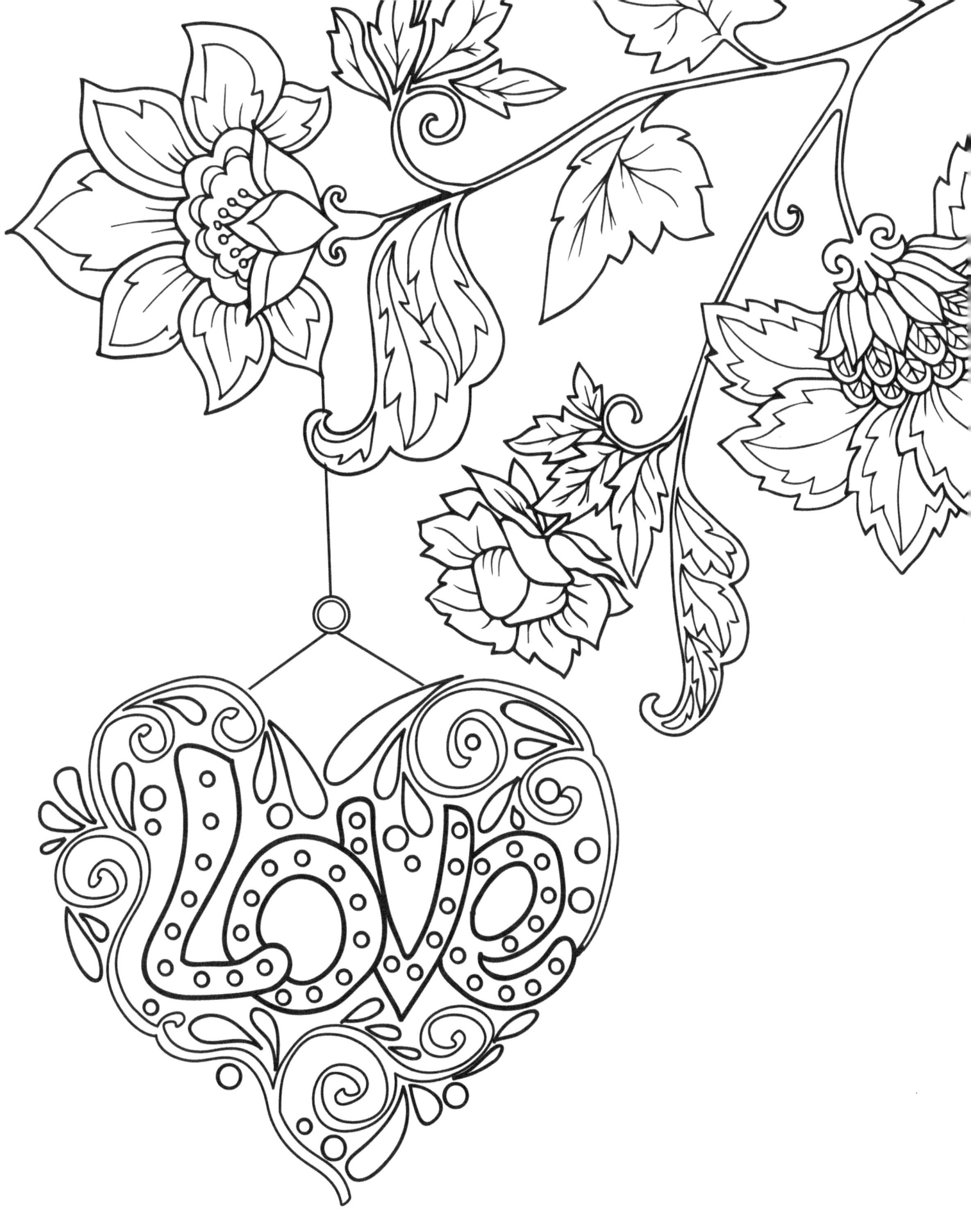

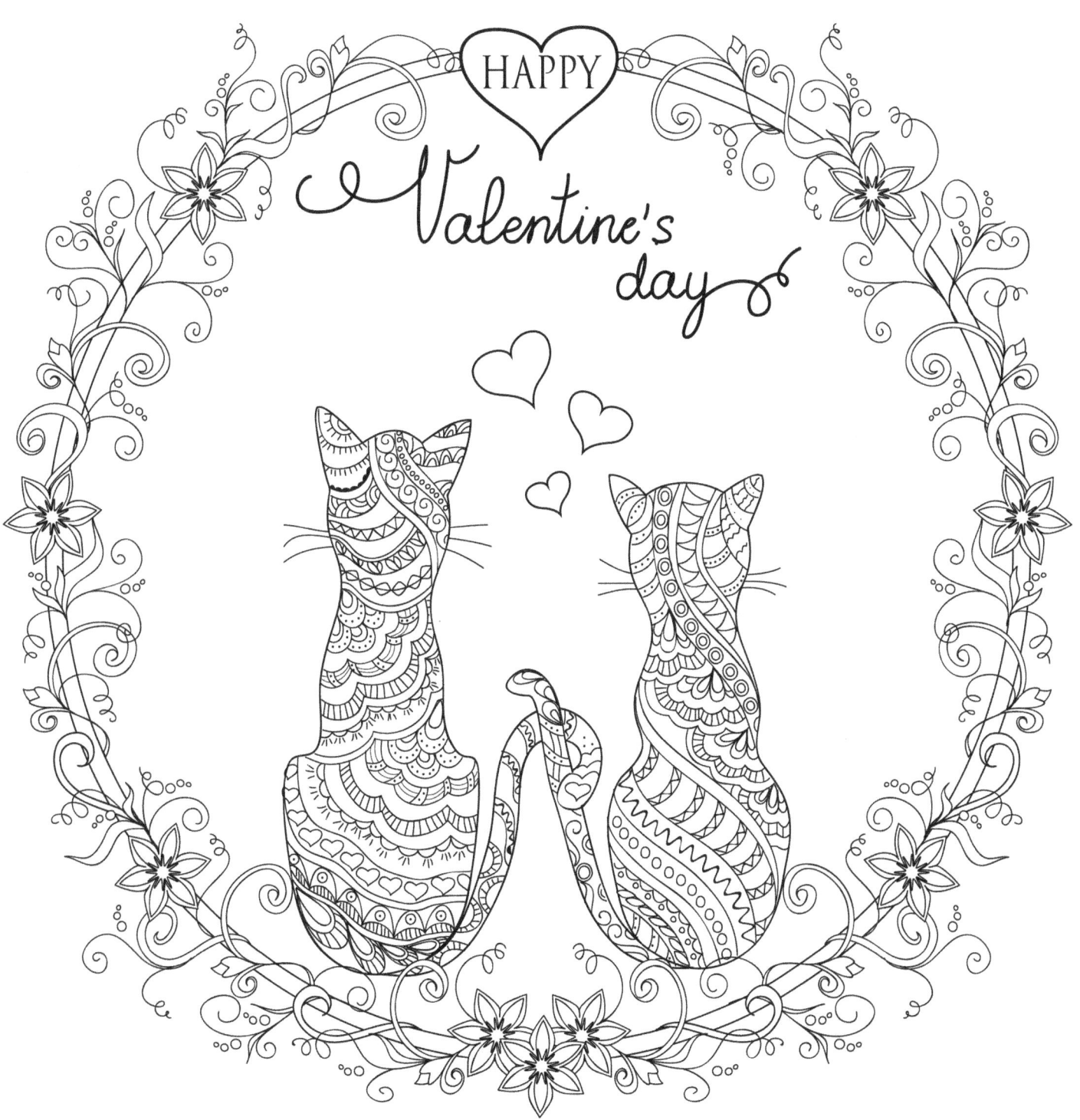

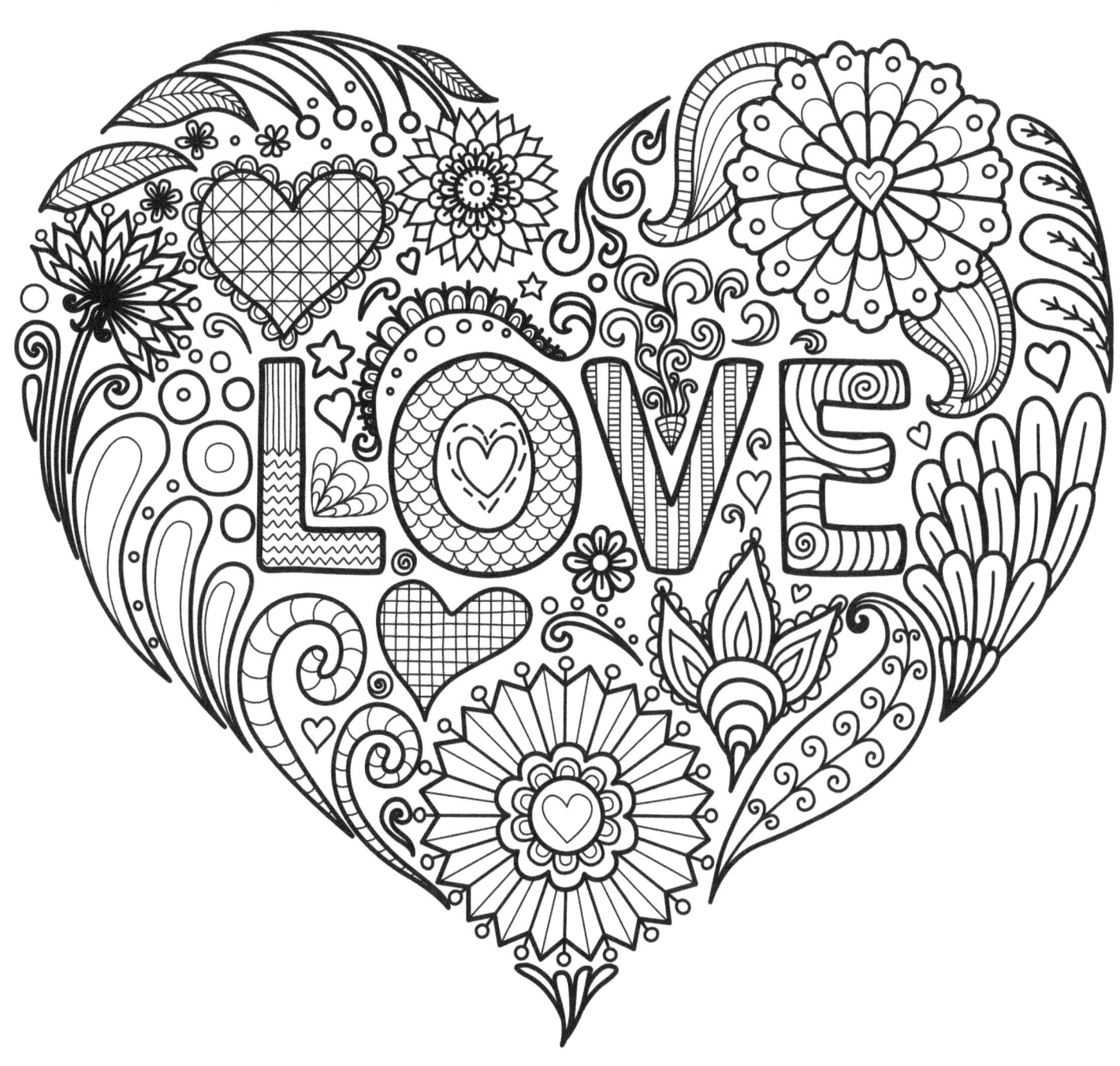

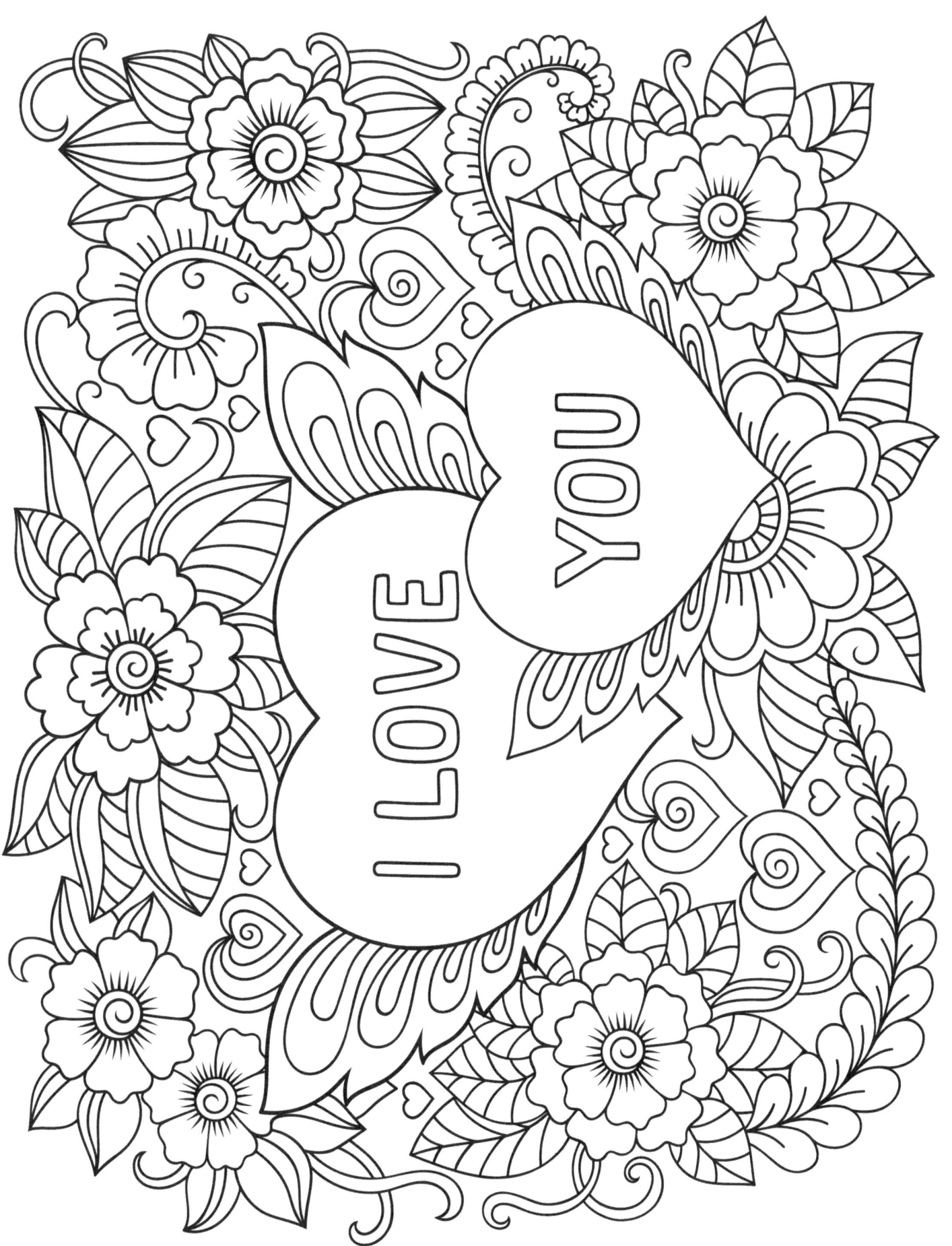

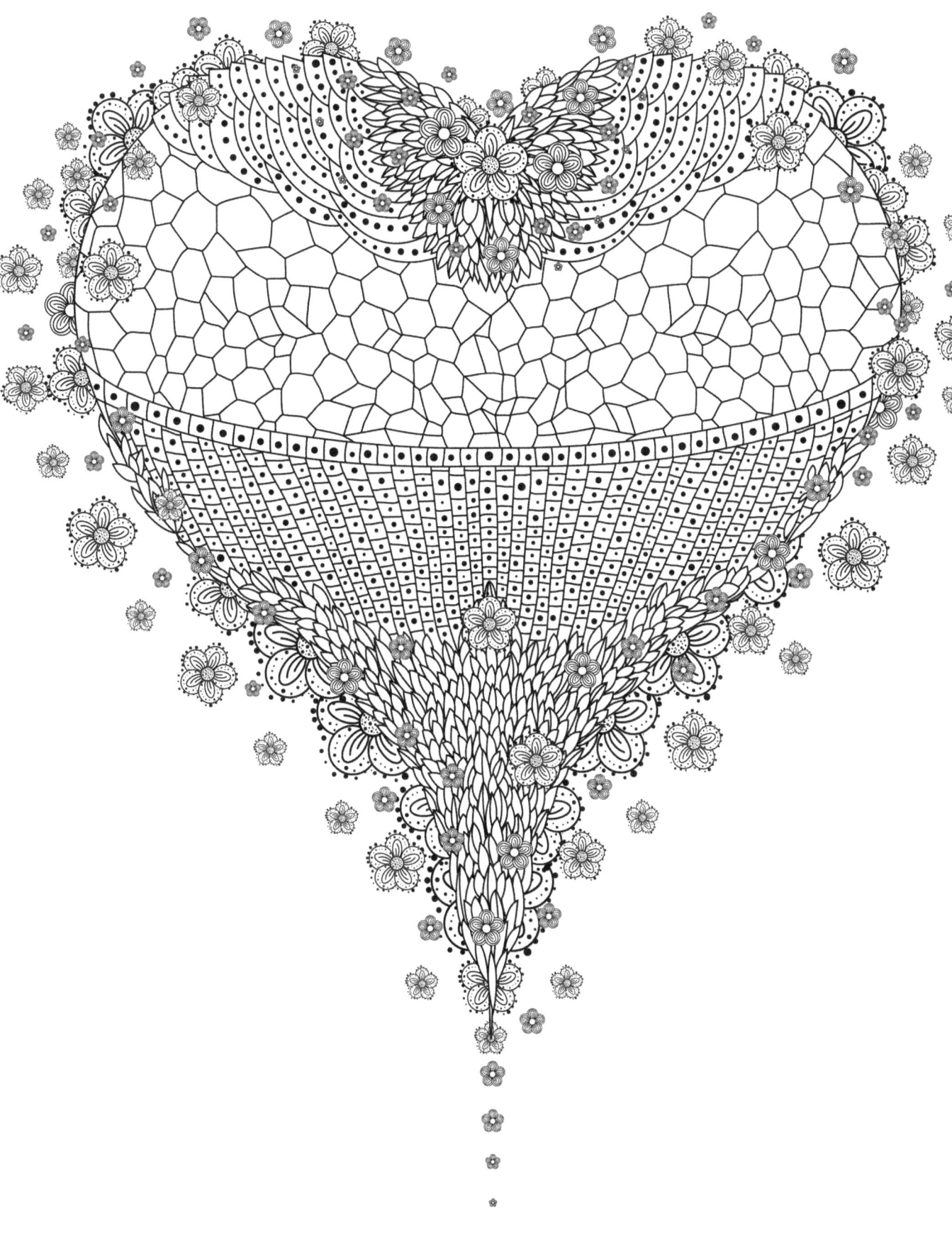

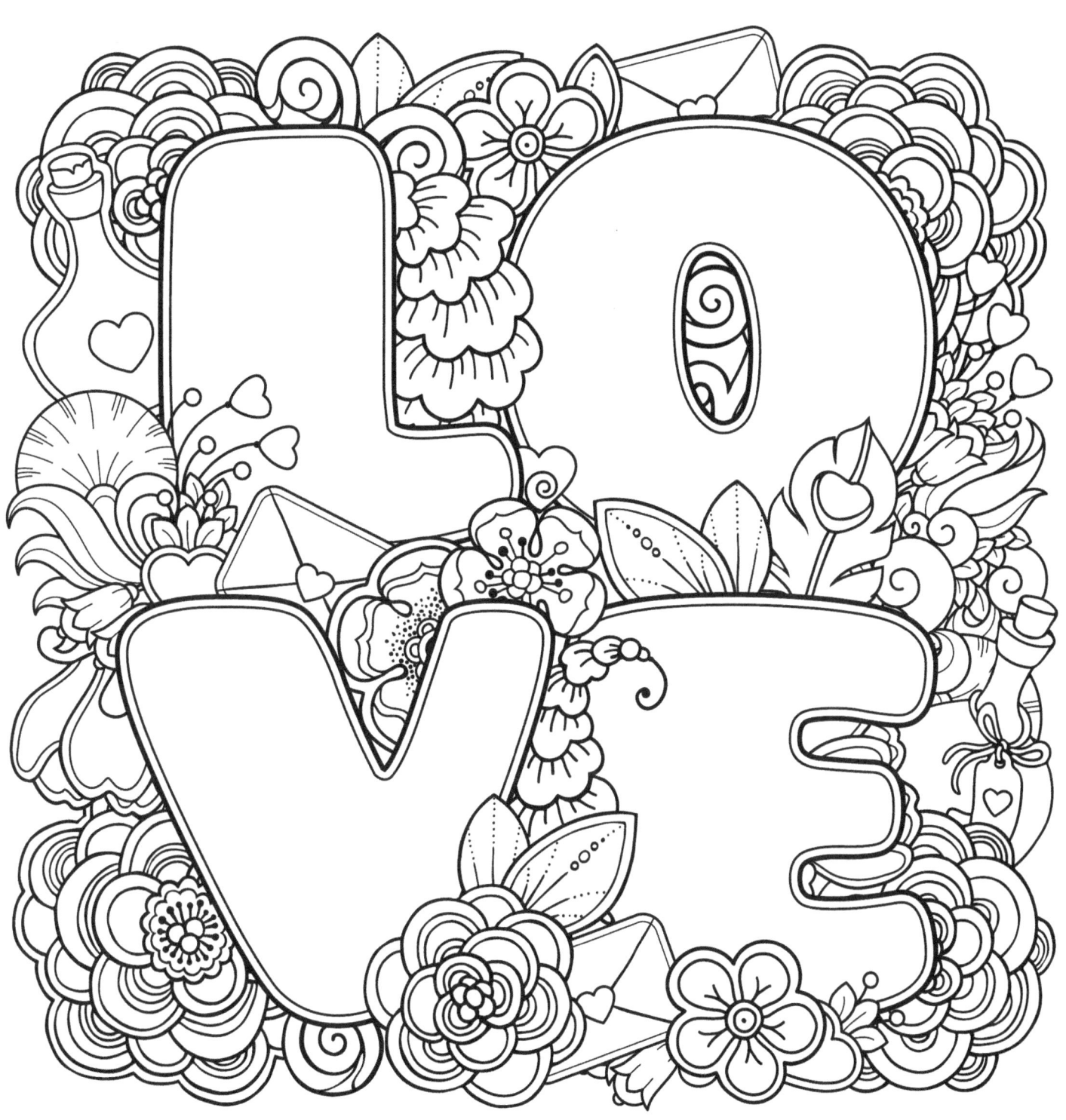

Happy Valentine's day

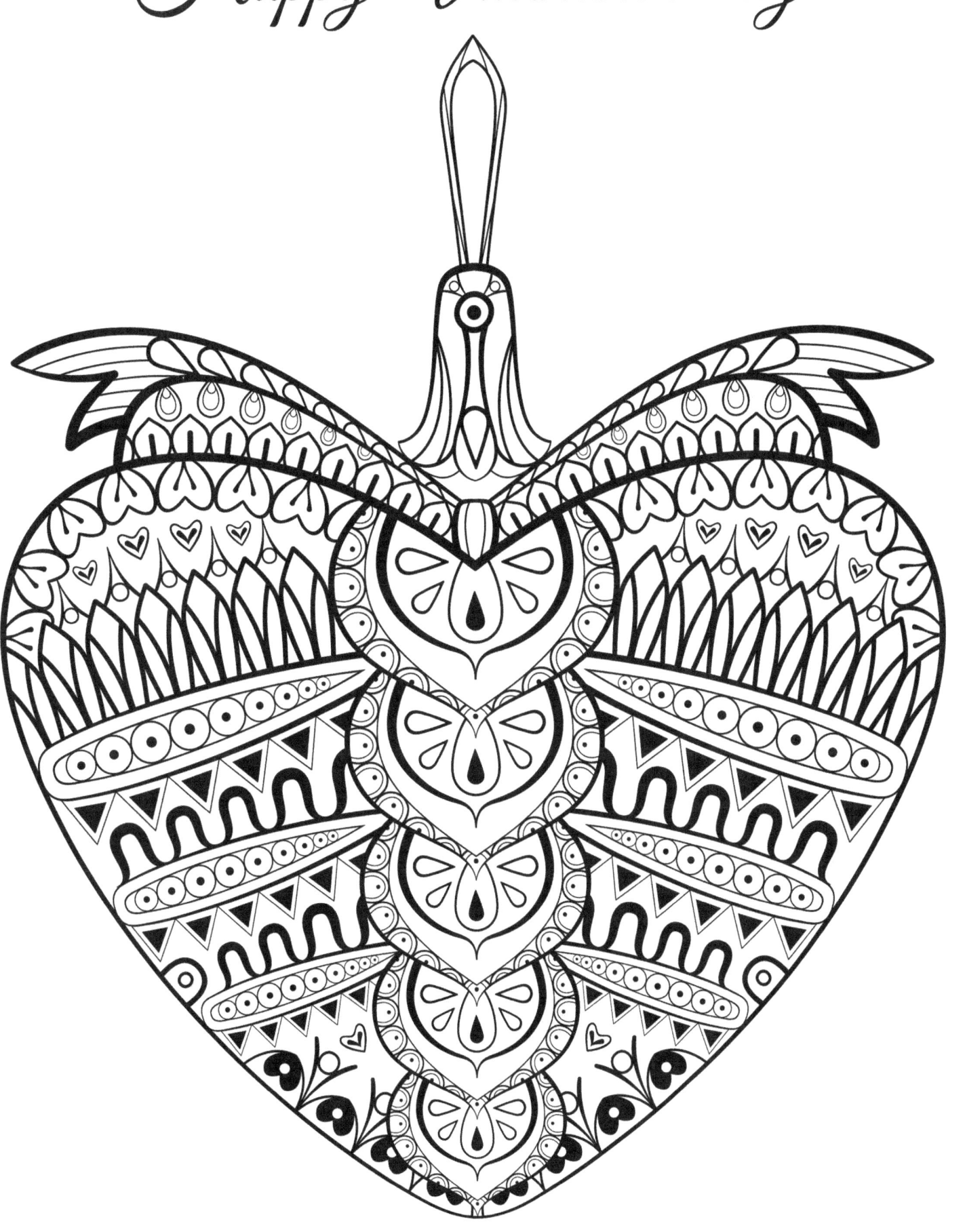

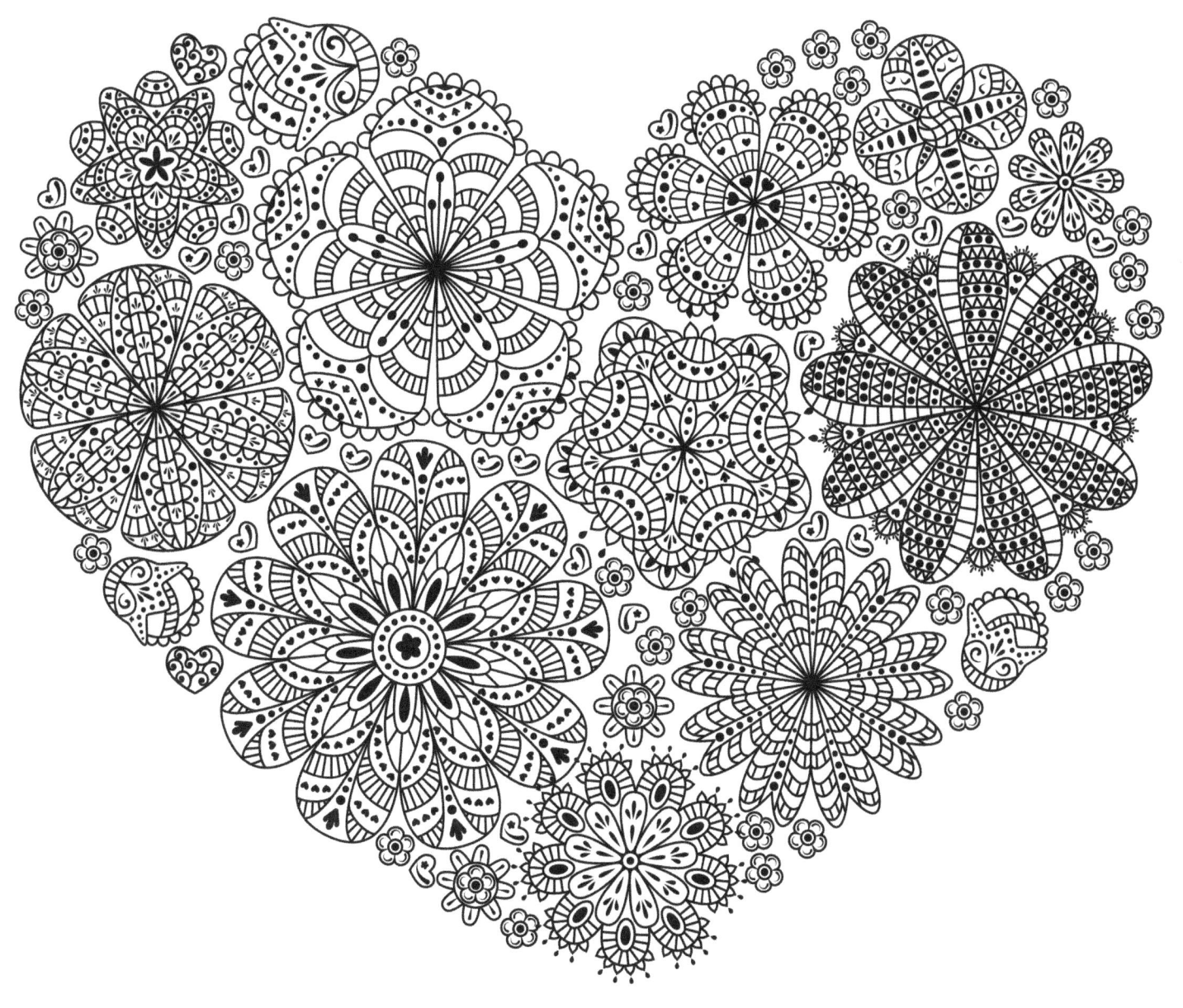

I love U

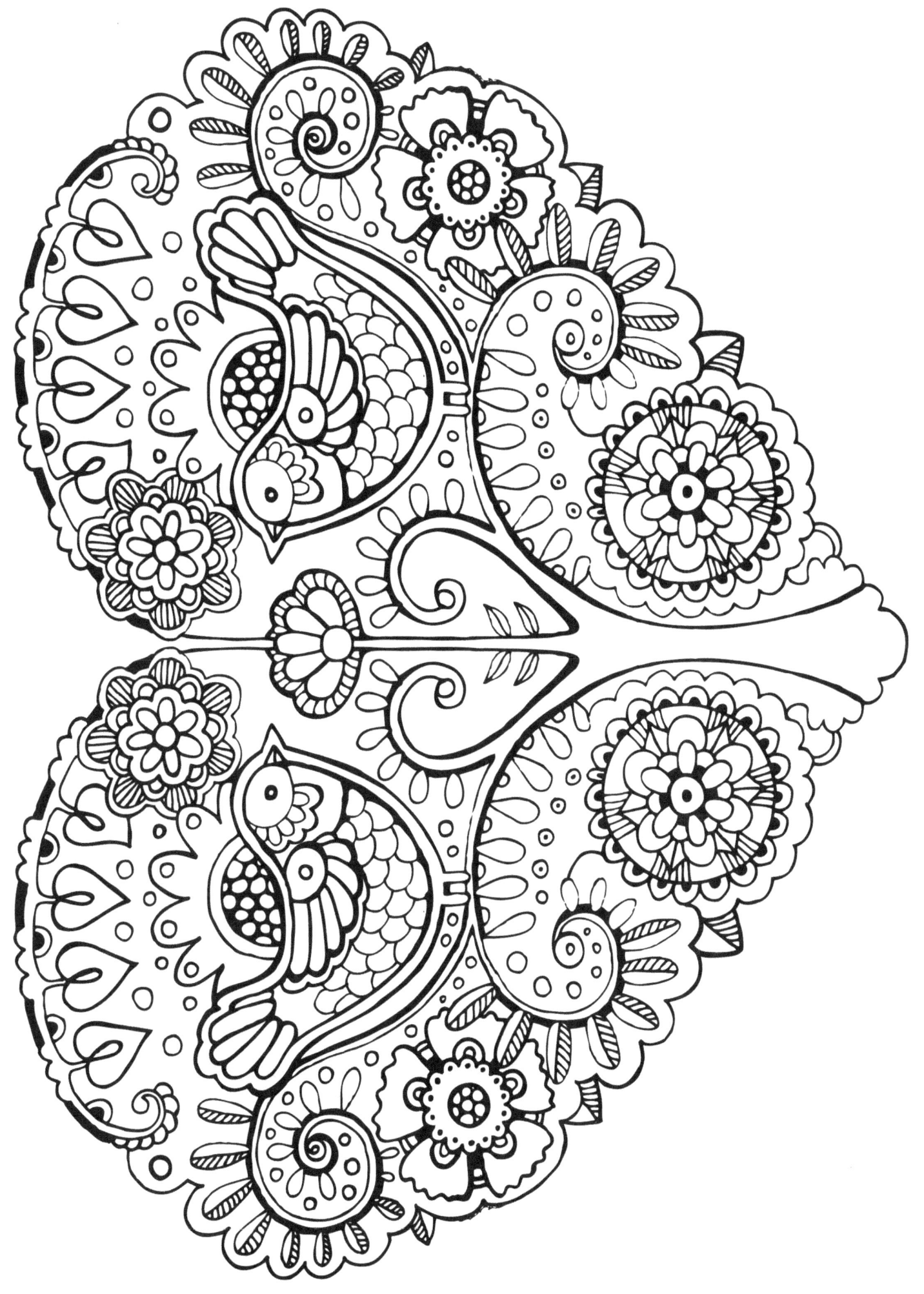

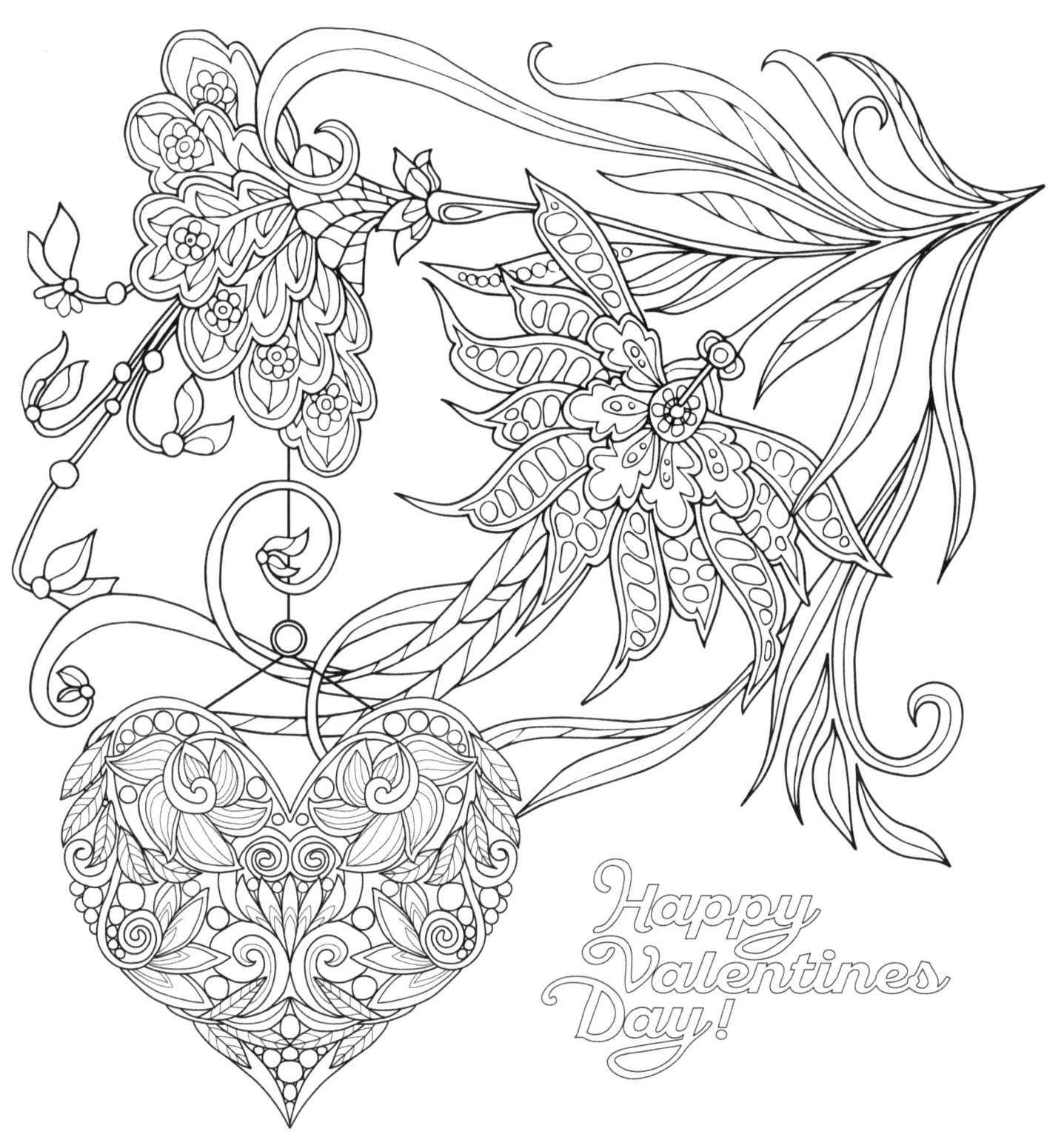

Happy
Valentines
Day!

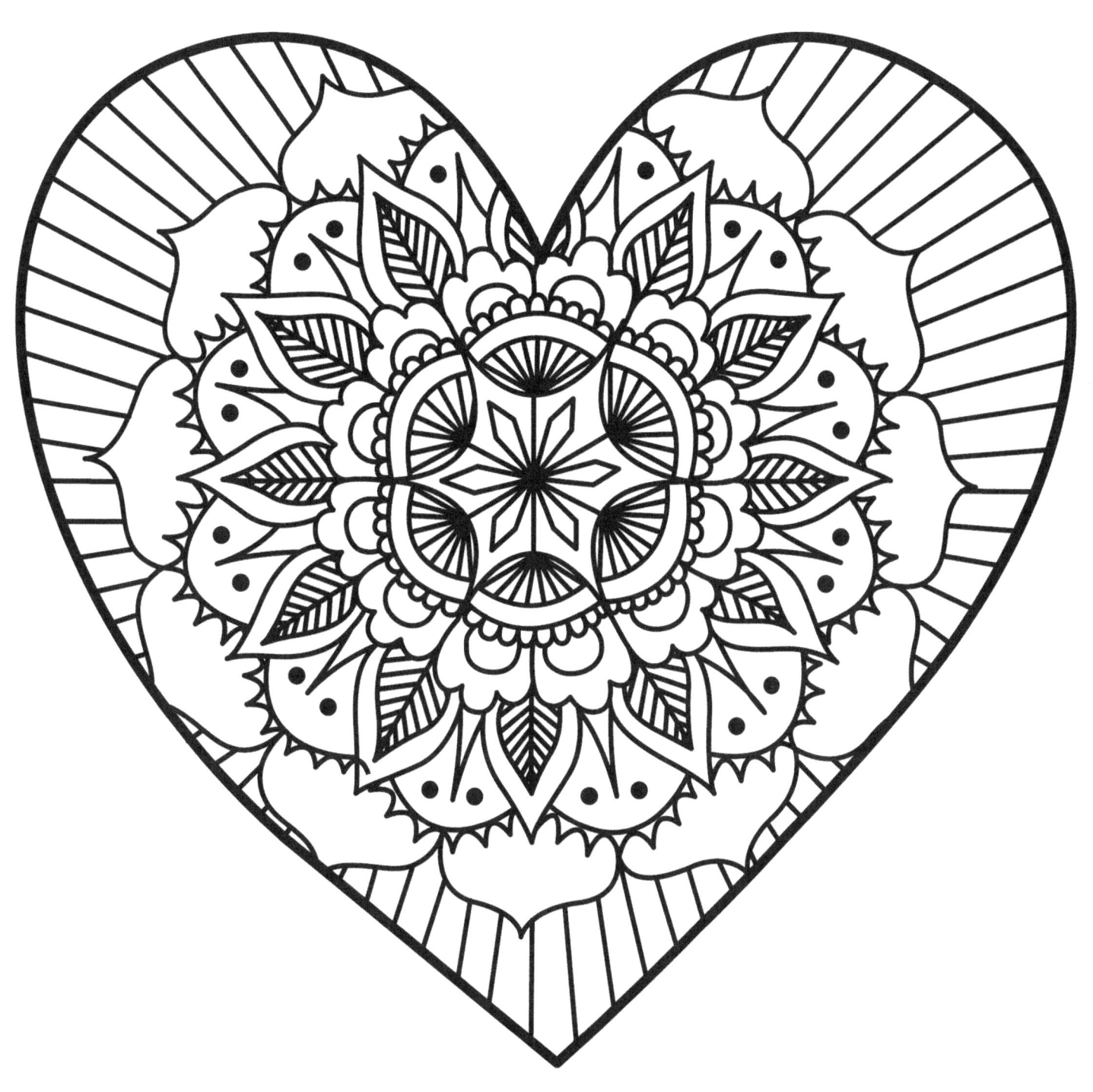

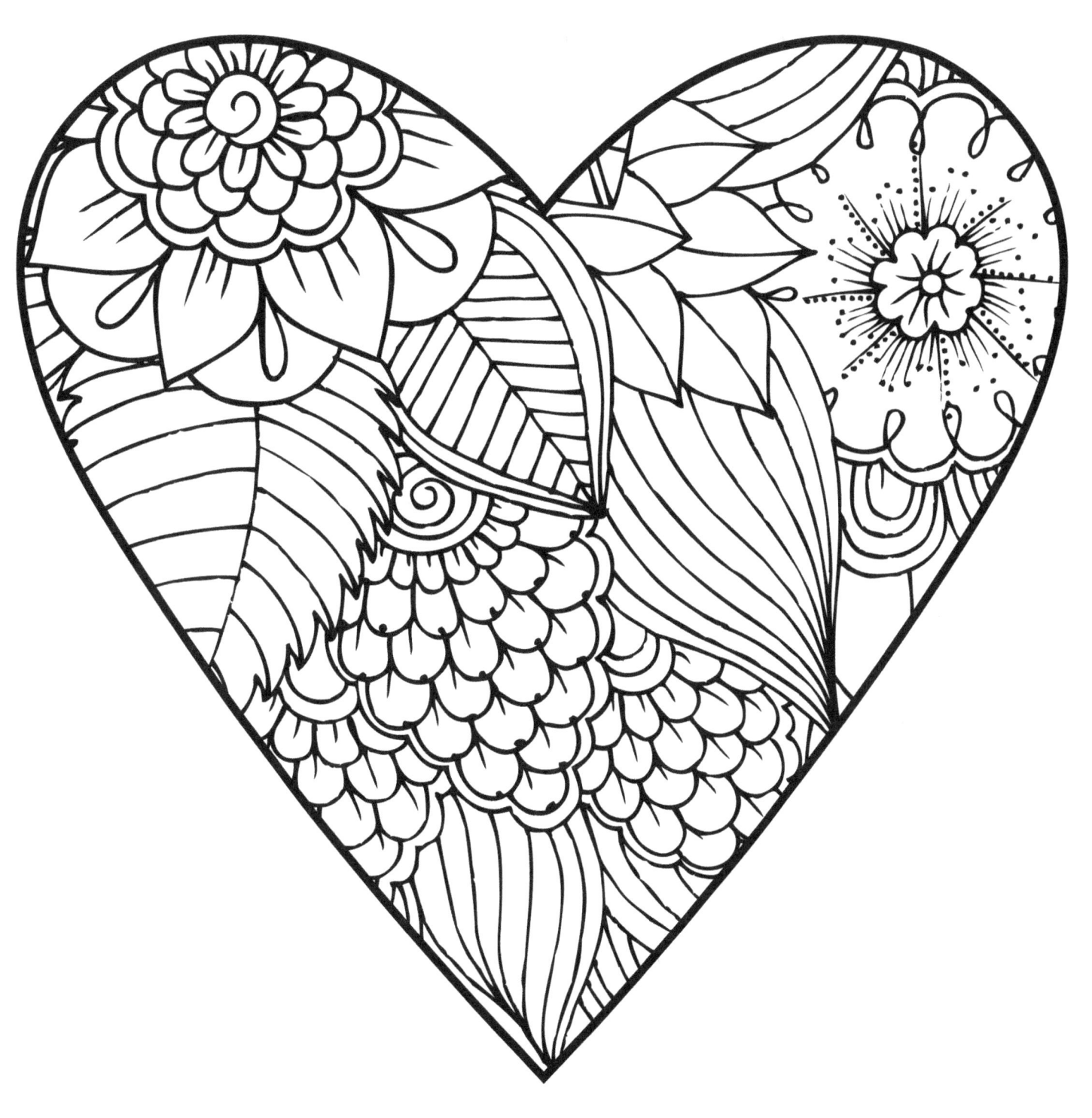

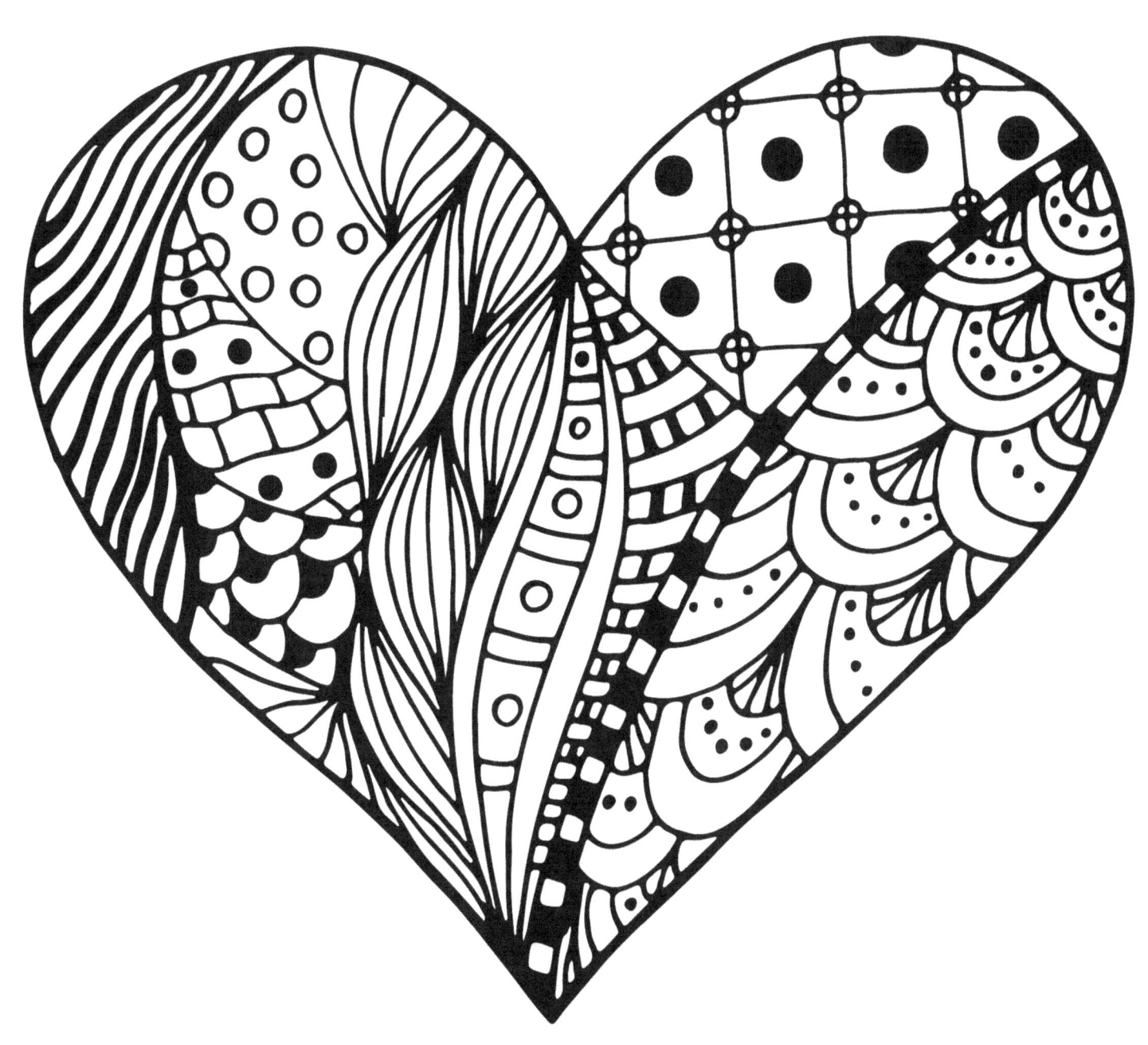

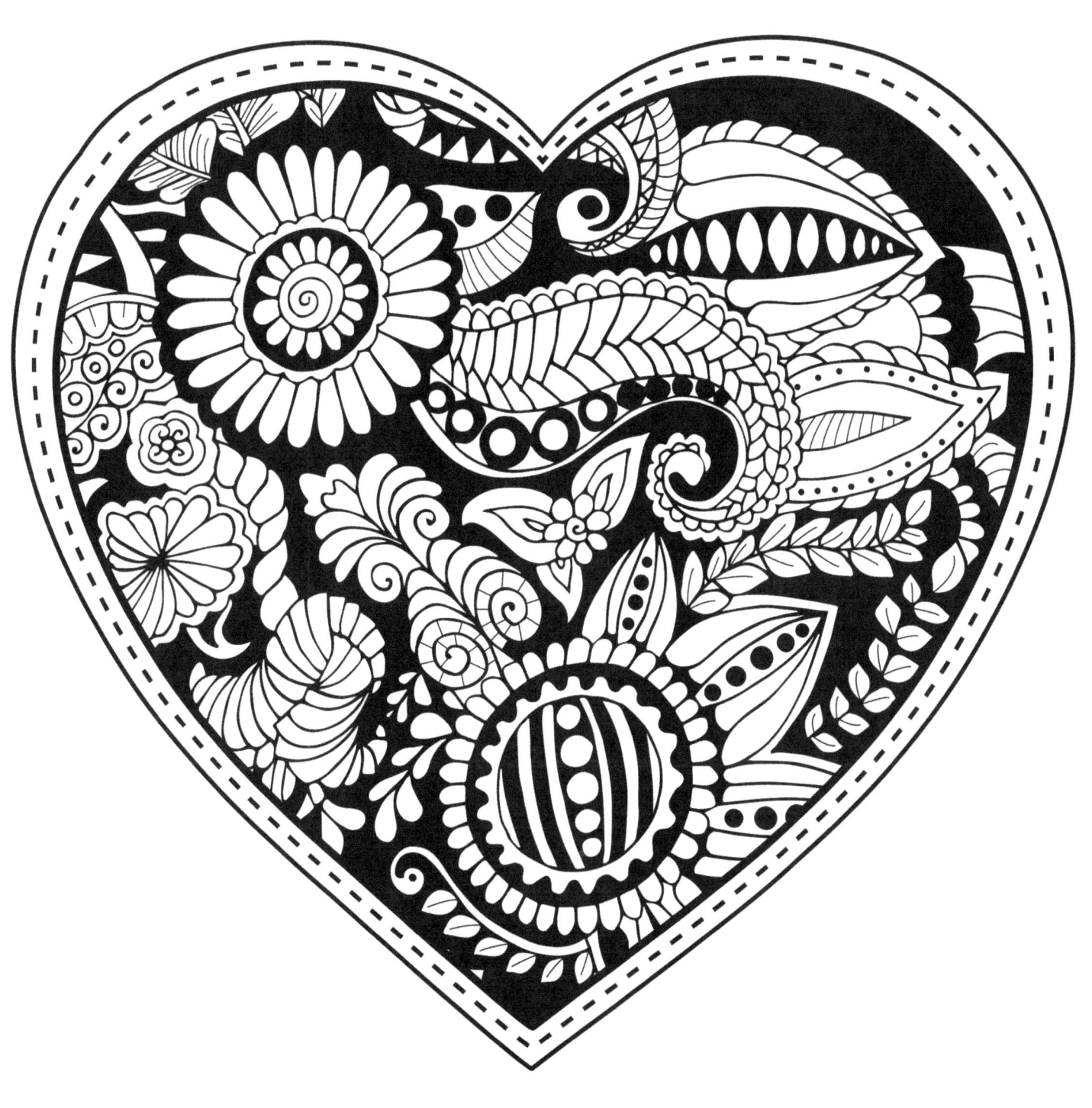

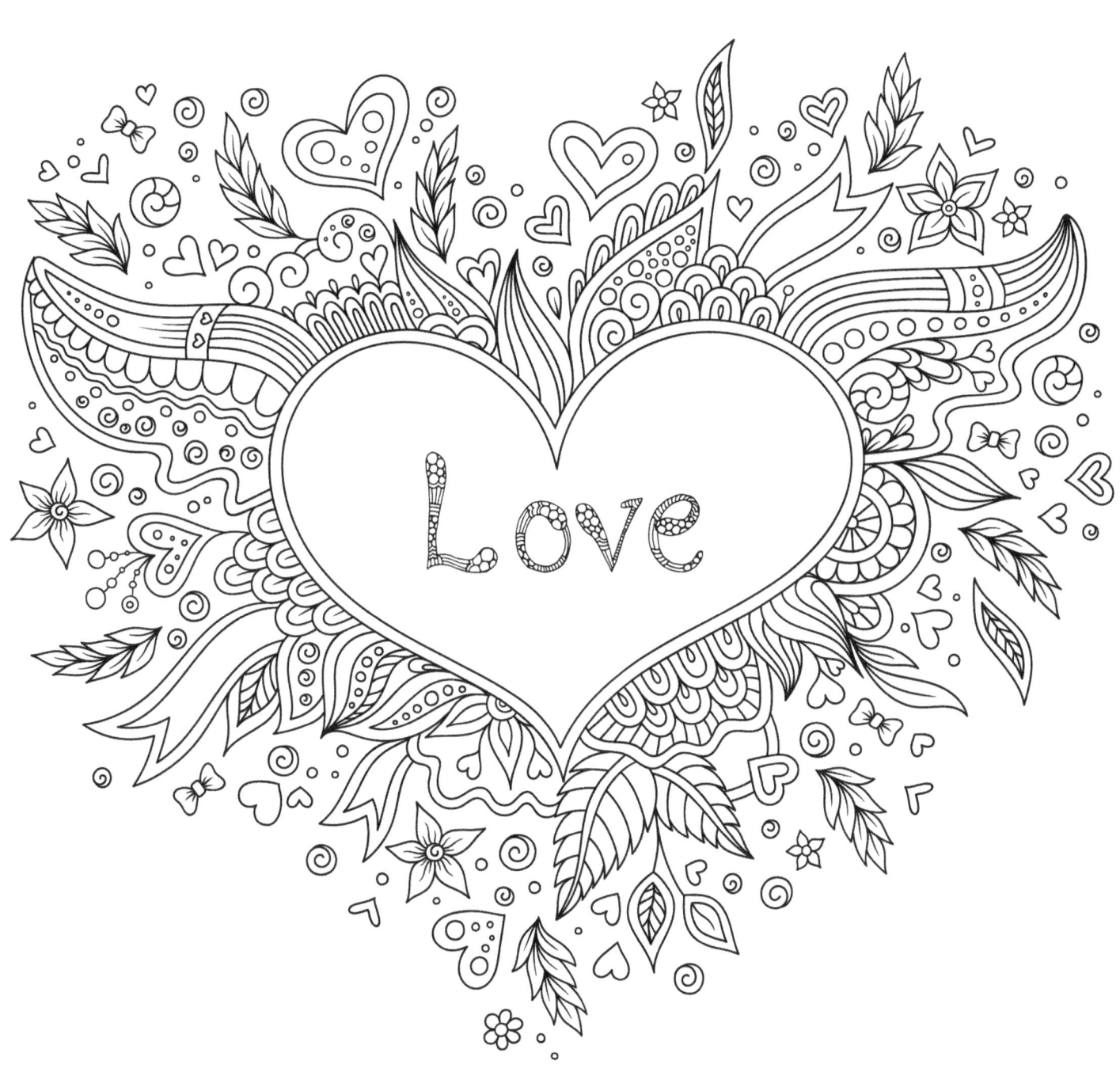

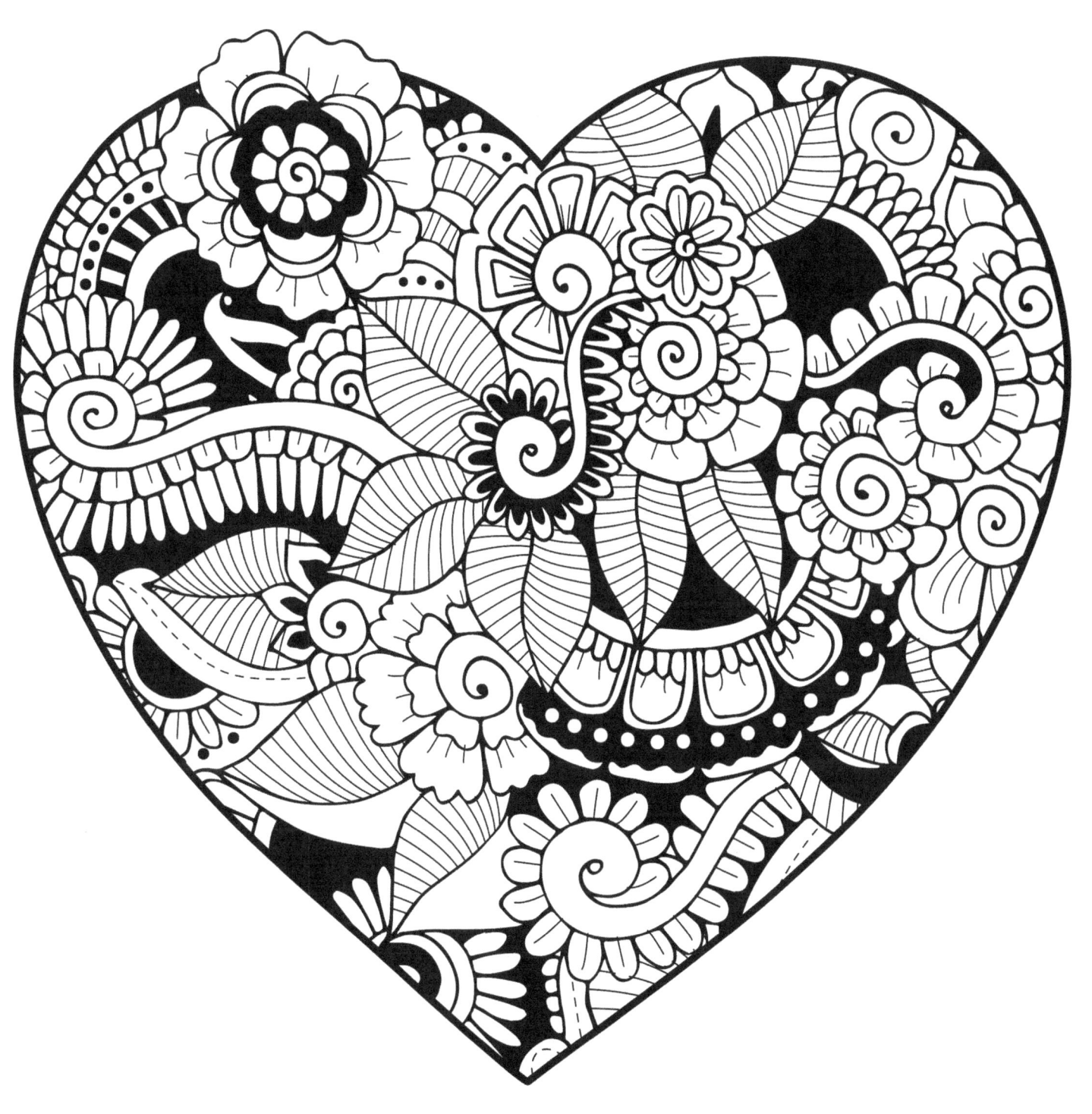

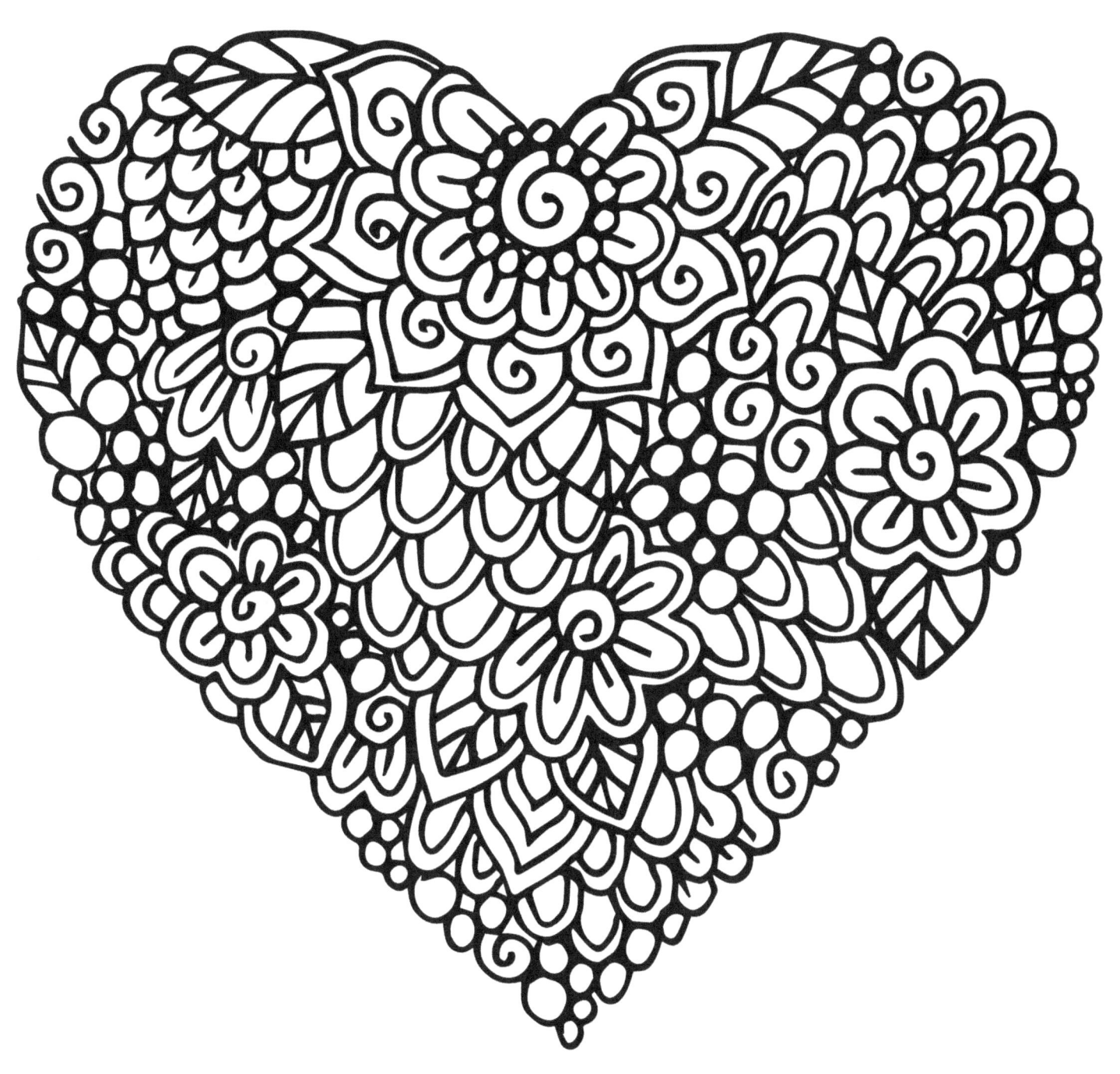

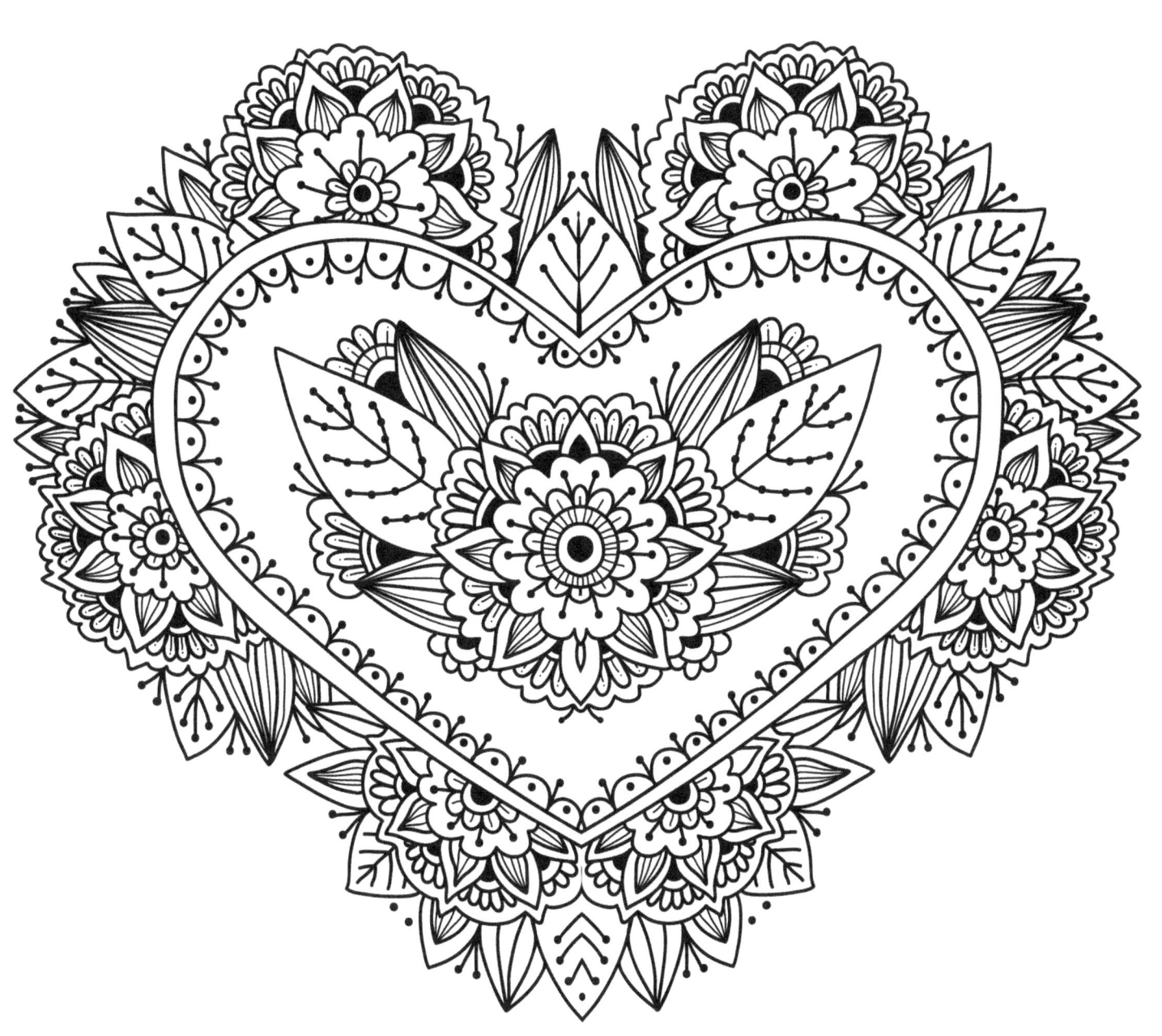

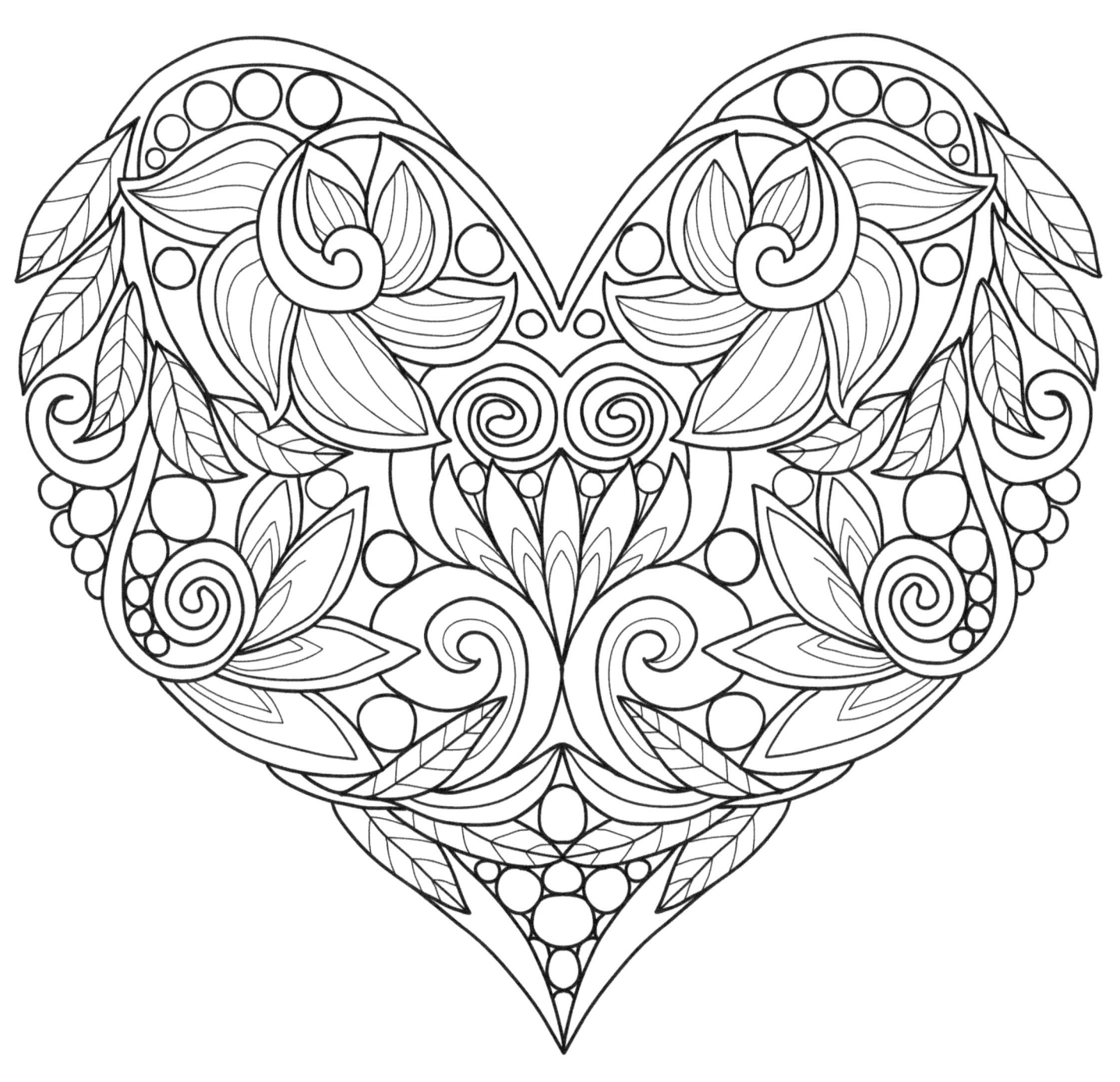

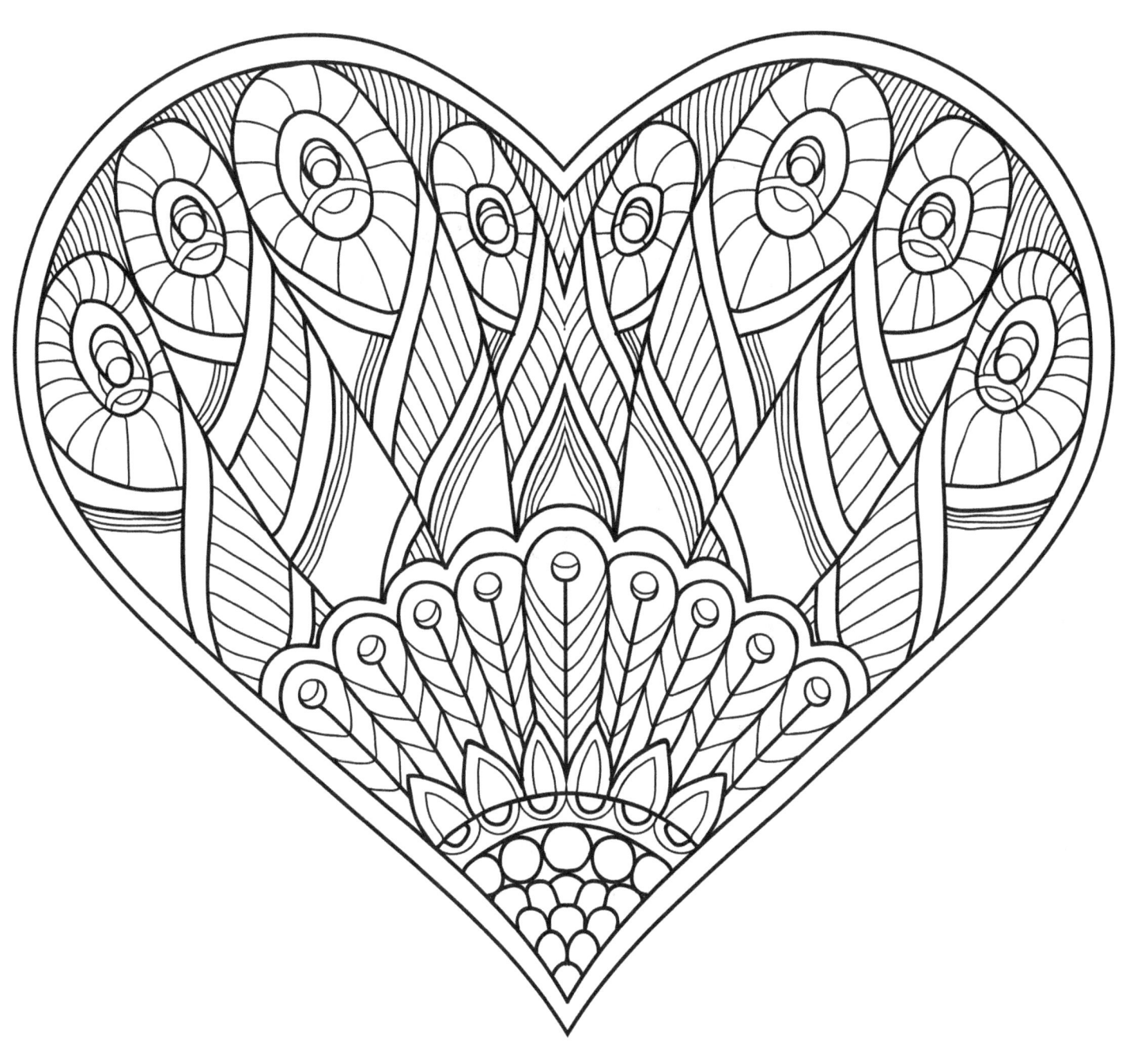

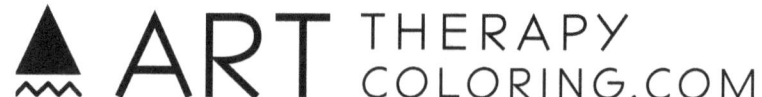

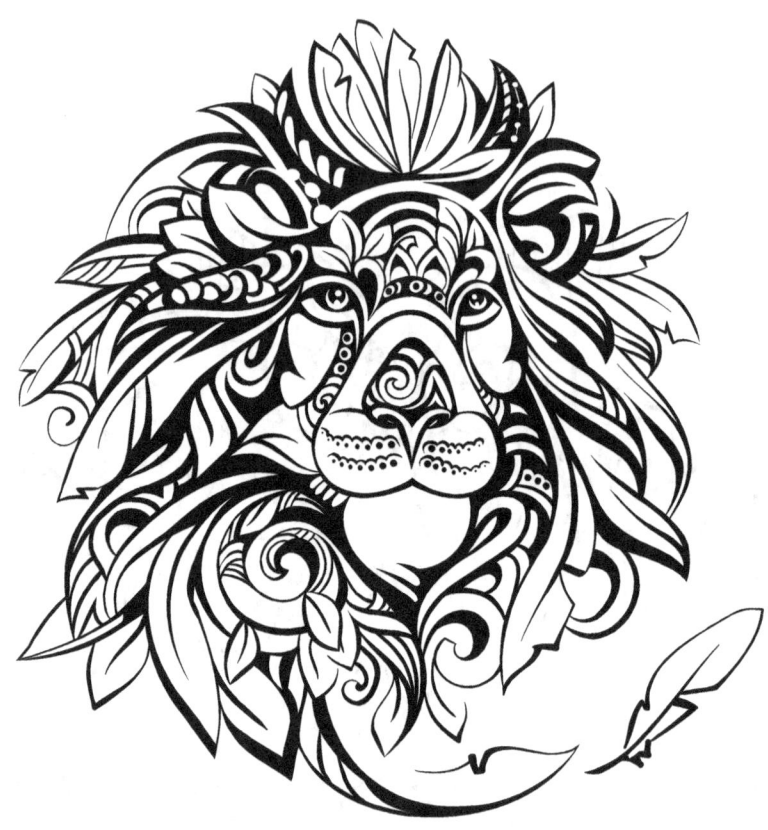

Did You Enjoy Our Coloring Book?

We Want To Hear About It!

Help spread the word about our coloring books! The best way to spread the word is through reviews. We know how busy you are, especially with all of that coloring, but we would appreciate it!

Visit our website at www.arttherapycoloring.com

Over 200 Art Therapy Coloring Books

See our collection of over 200 Art Therapy Coloring Books for Adults, Men, Women, Seniors, Teens, Kids, Boys, and Girls.

Coloring Books For Adults

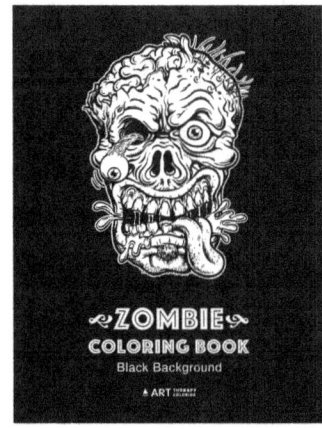

ZOMBIE
COLORING BOOK
Black Background

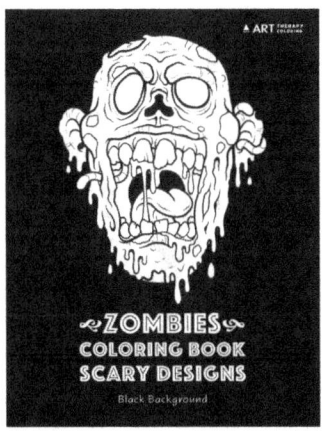

ZOMBIES
COLORING BOOK
SCARY DESIGNS
Black Background

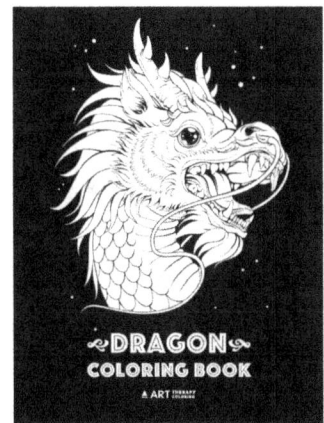

DRAGON
COLORING BOOK

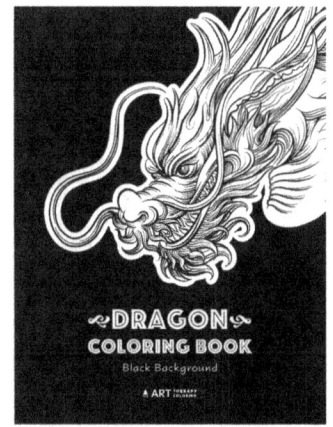

DRAGON
COLORING BOOK
Black Background

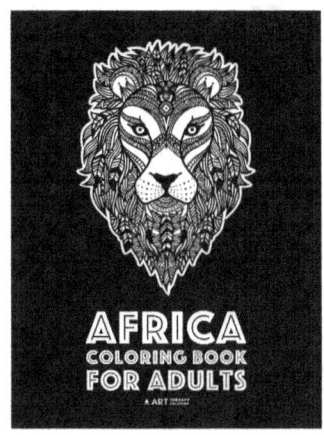

AFRICA
COLORING BOOK
FOR ADULTS

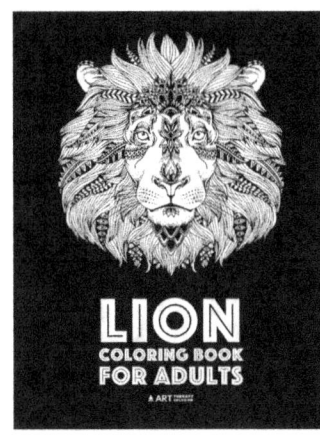

LION
COLORING BOOK
FOR ADULTS

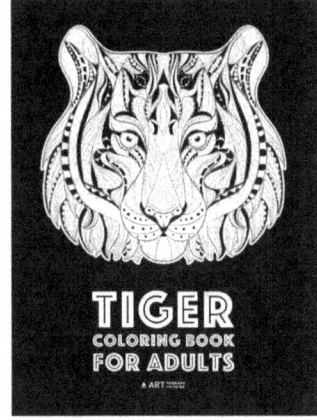

TIGER
COLORING BOOK
FOR ADULTS

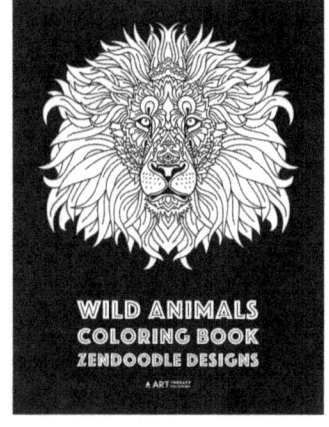

WILD ANIMALS
COLORING BOOK
ZENDOODLE DESIGNS

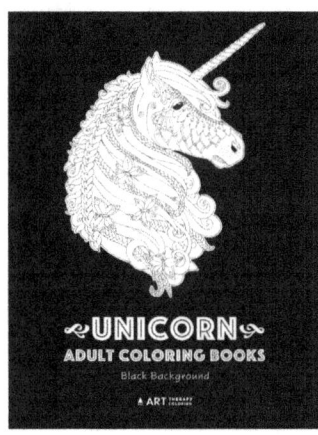

UNICORN
ADULT COLORING BOOKS
Black Background

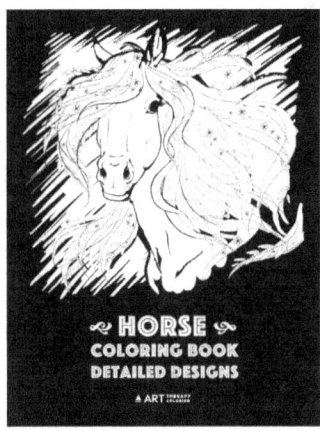

HORSE
COLORING BOOK
DETAILED DESIGNS

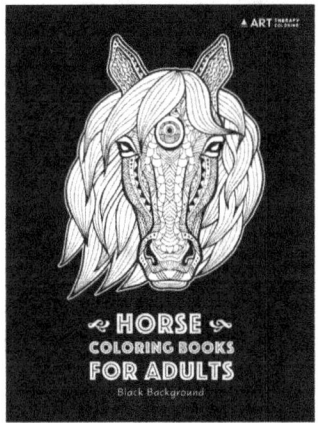

HORSE
COLORING BOOKS
FOR ADULTS
Black Background

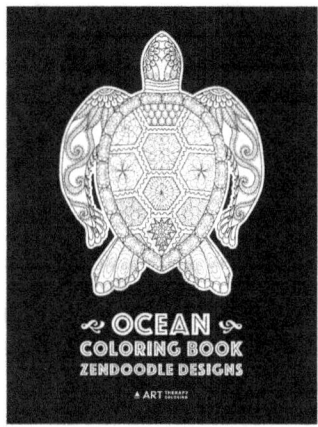

OCEAN
COLORING BOOK
ZENDOODLE DESIGNS

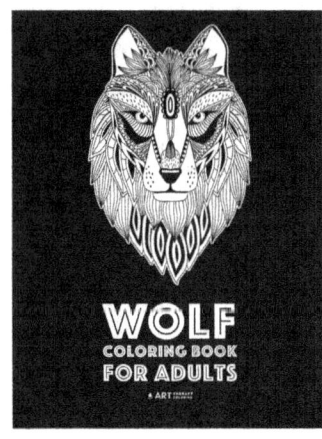

WOLF
COLORING BOOK
FOR ADULTS

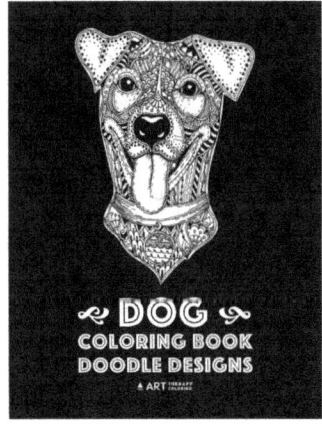

DOG
COLORING BOOK
DOODLE DESIGNS

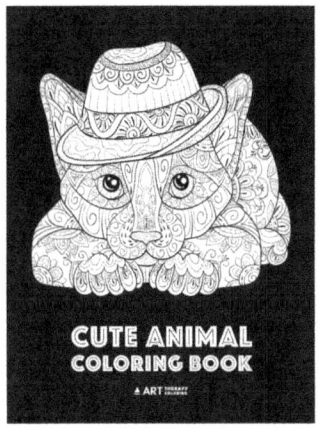

CUTE ANIMAL
COLORING BOOK

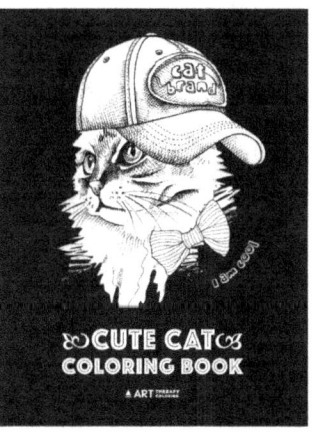

CUTE CAT
COLORING BOOK

Coloring Books For Adults

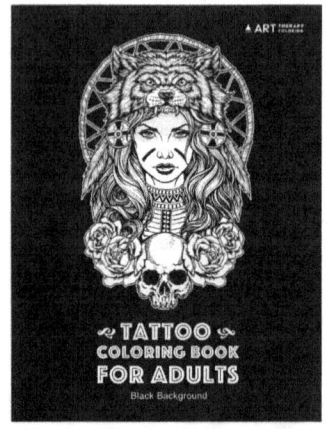

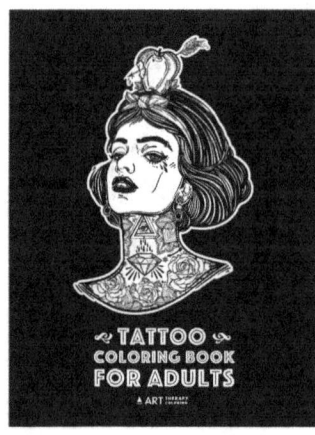

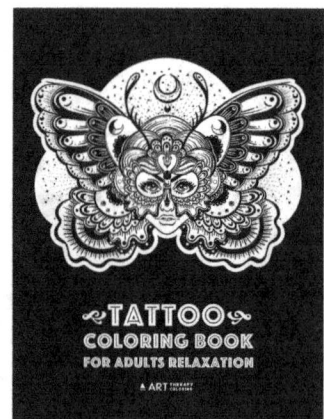

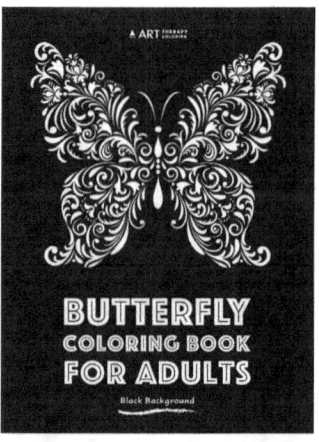

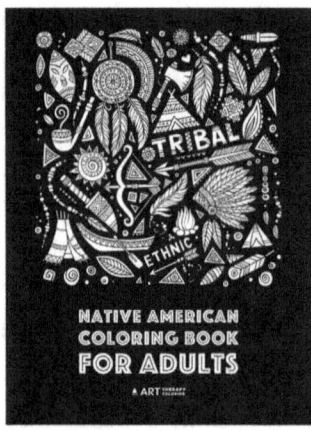

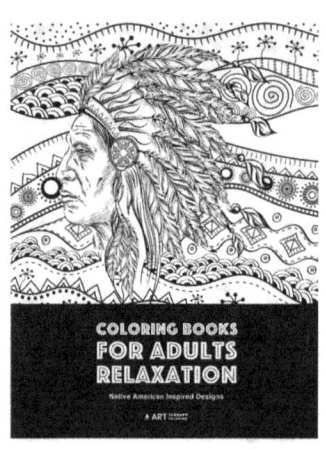

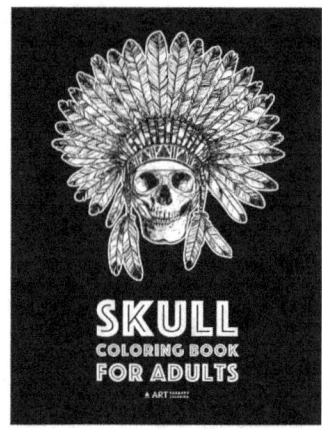

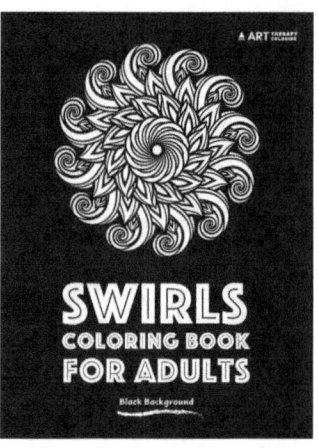

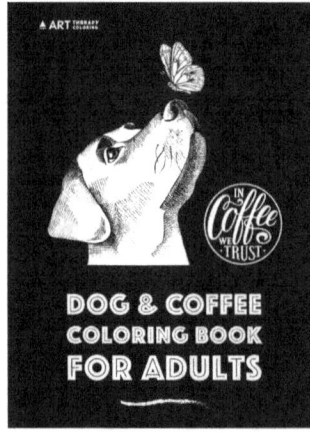

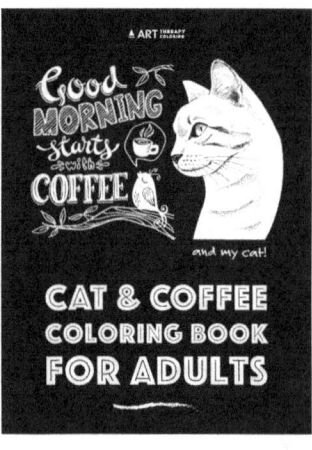

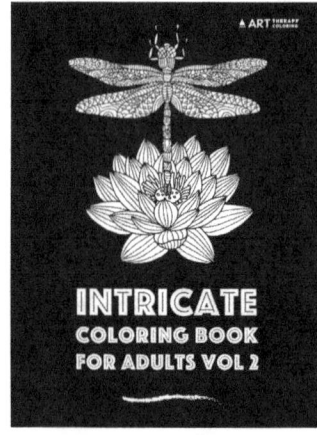

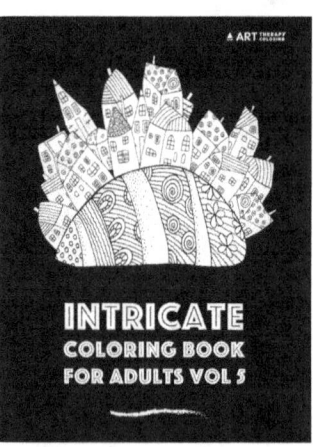

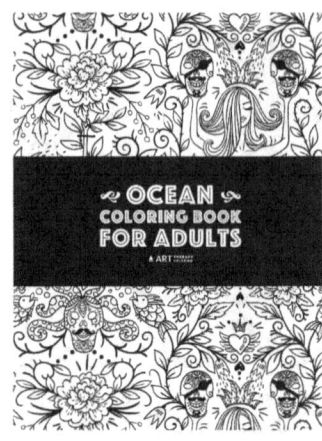

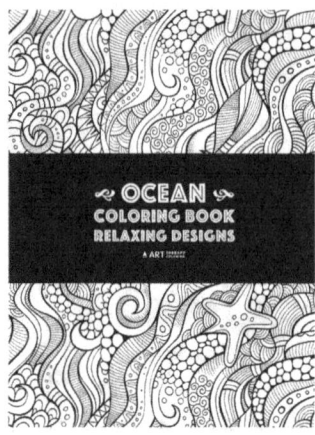

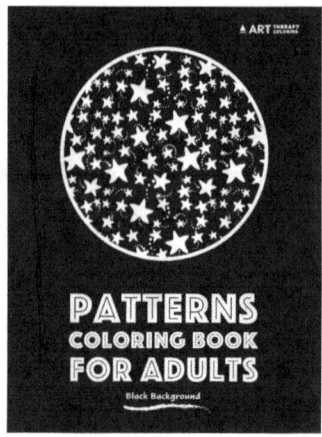

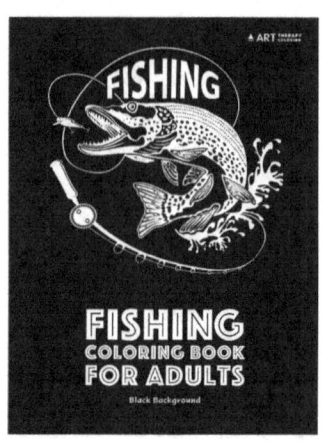

Coloring Books For Adults

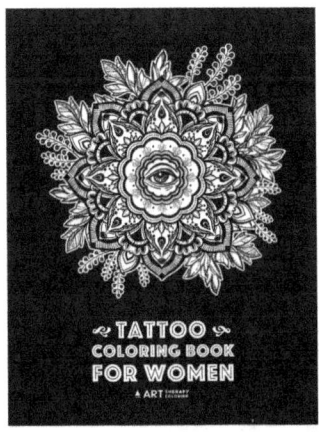

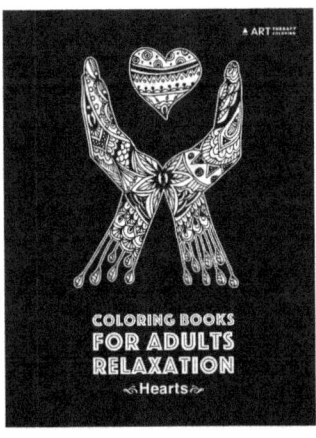

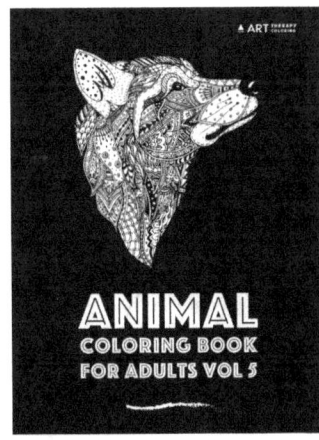

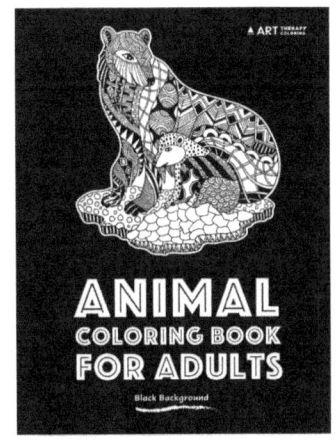

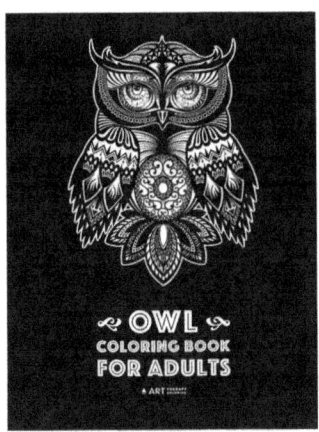

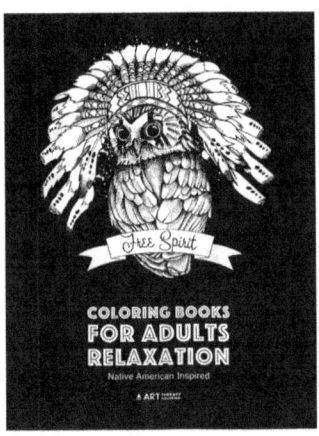

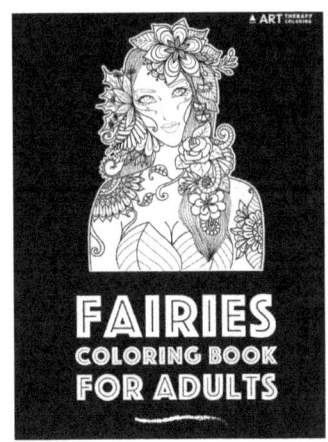

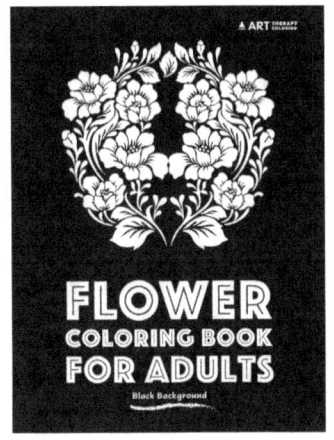

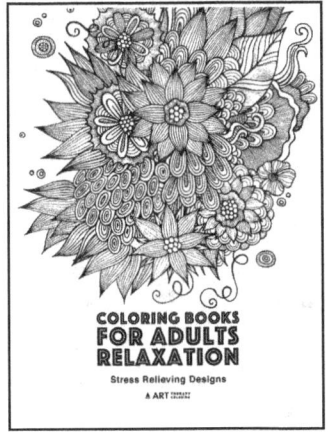

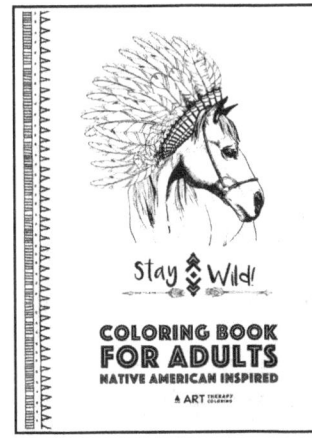

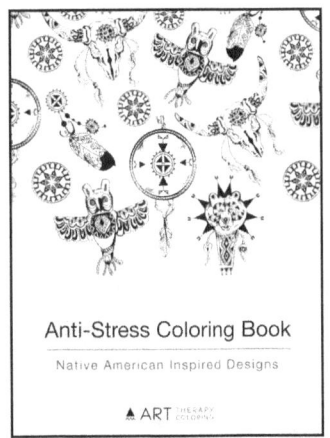

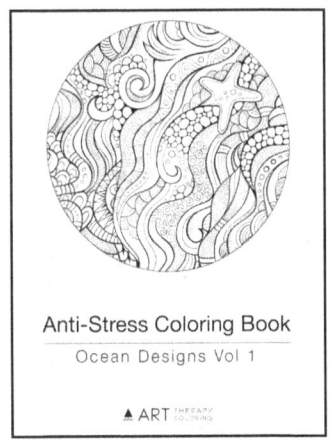

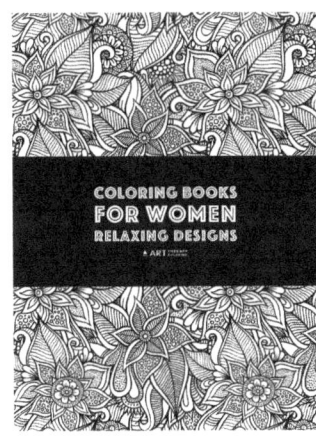

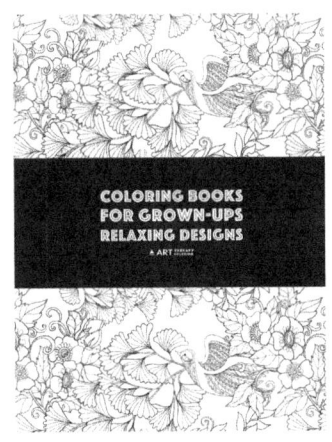

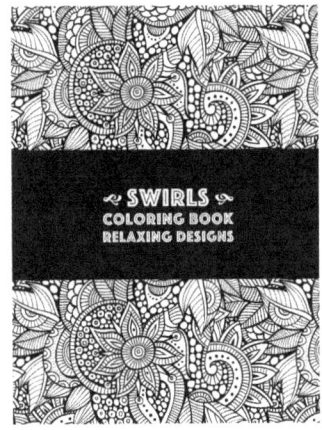

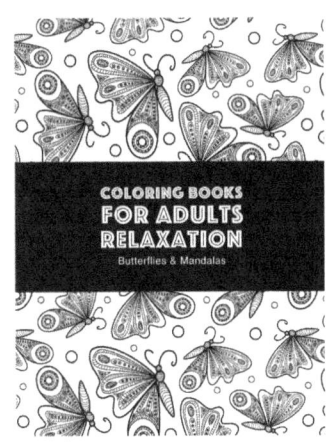

Coloring Books For Men

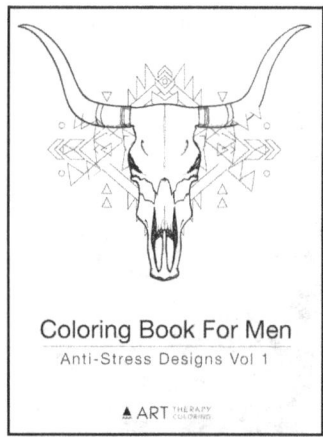

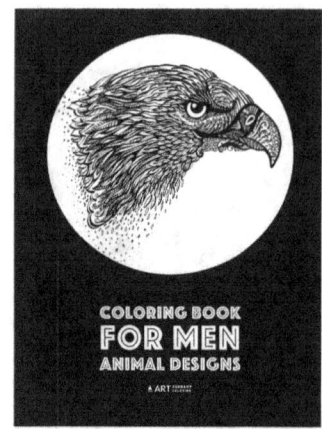

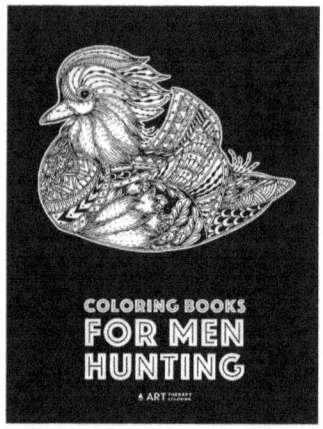

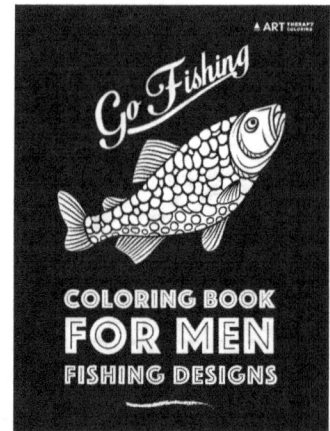

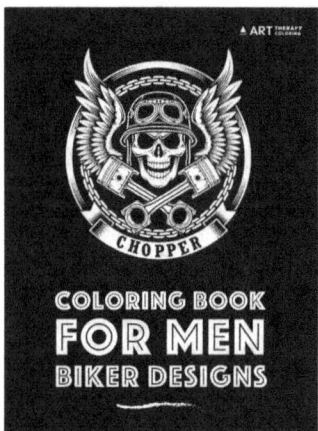

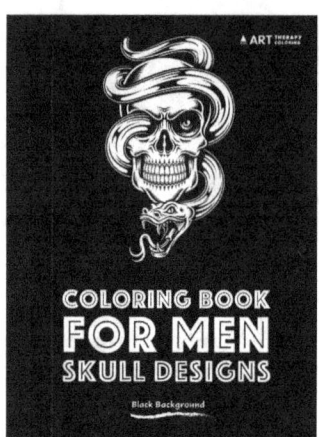

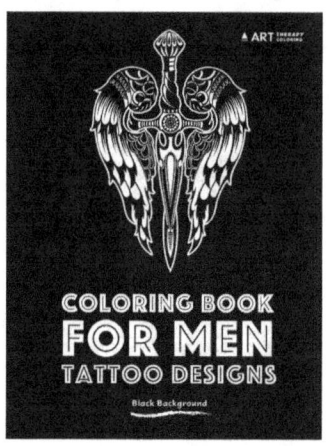

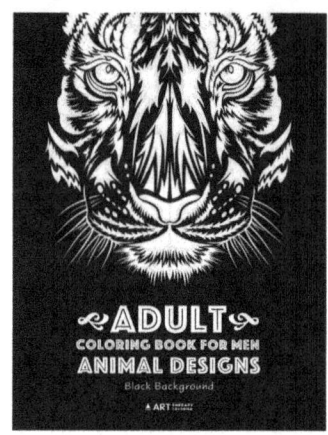

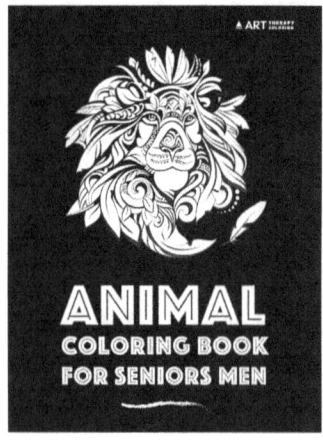

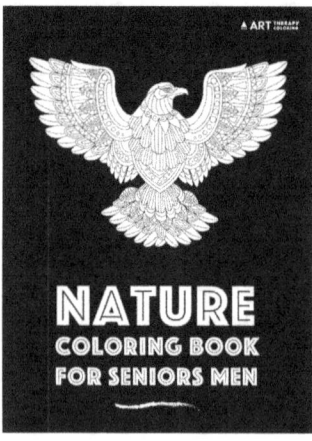

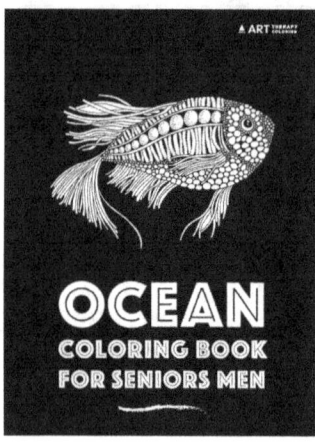

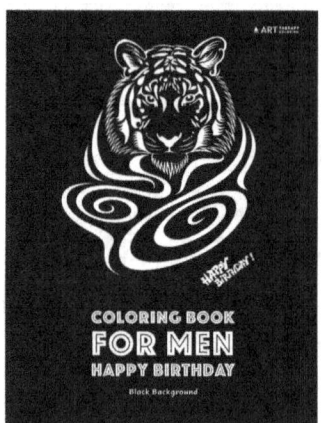

Coloring Books For Seniors

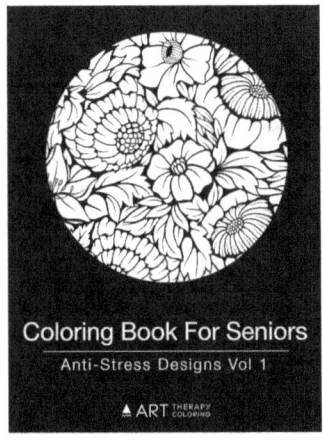

Coloring Book For Seniors
Anti-Stress Designs Vol 1

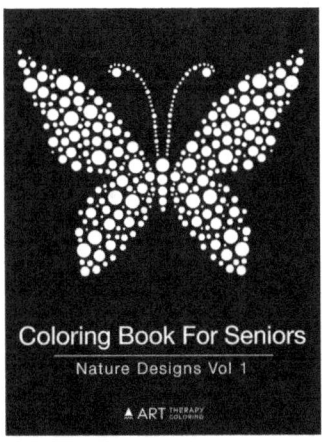

Coloring Book For Seniors
Nature Designs Vol 1

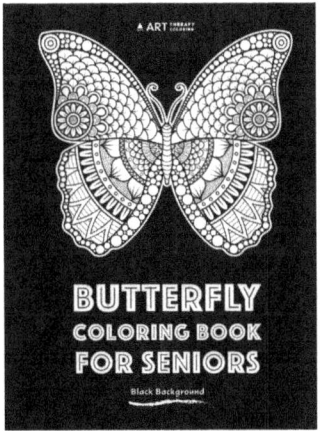

BUTTERFLY COLORING BOOK FOR SENIORS
Black Background

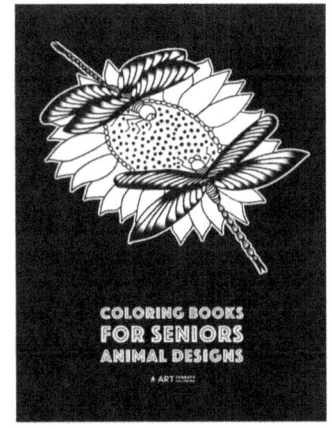

COLORING BOOKS FOR SENIORS ANIMAL DESIGNS

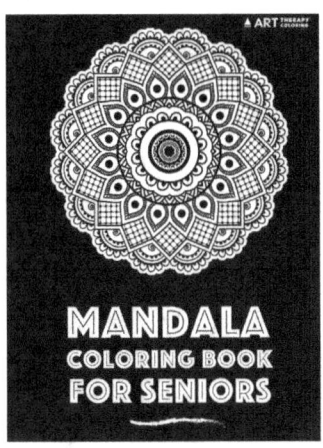

MANDALA COLORING BOOK FOR SENIORS

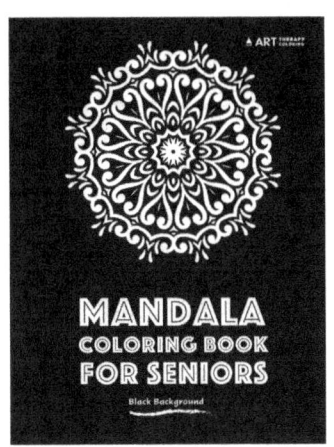

MANDALA COLORING BOOK FOR SENIORS
Black Background

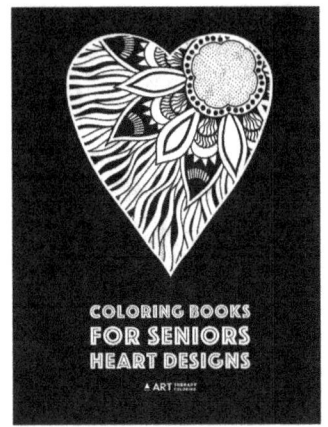

COLORING BOOKS FOR SENIORS HEART DESIGNS

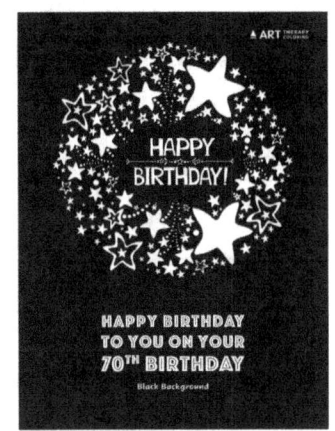

HAPPY BIRTHDAY!
HAPPY BIRTHDAY TO YOU ON YOUR 70TH BIRTHDAY
Black Background

COLORING BOOKS FOR SENIORS SWIRL DESIGNS
Black Background

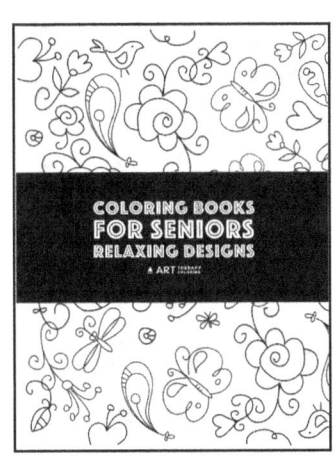

COLORING BOOKS FOR SENIORS RELAXING DESIGNS

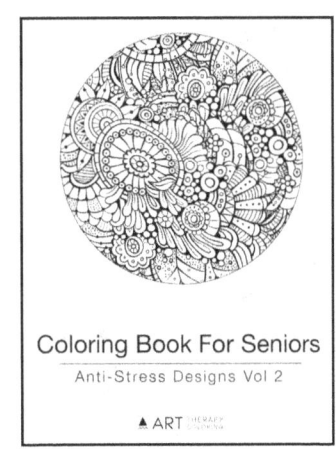

Coloring Book For Seniors
Anti-Stress Designs Vol 2

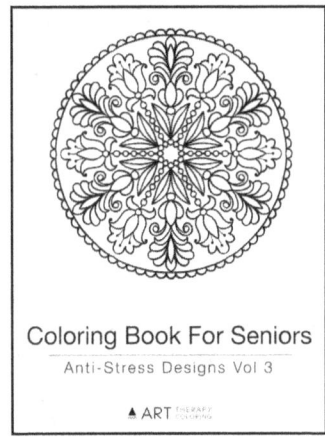

Coloring Book For Seniors
Anti-Stress Designs Vol 3

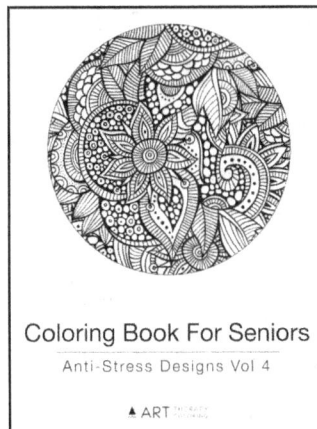

Coloring Book For Seniors
Anti-Stress Designs Vol 4

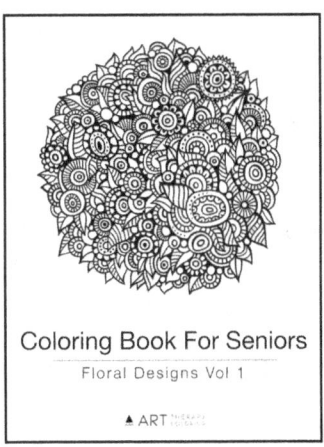

Coloring Book For Seniors
Floral Designs Vol 1

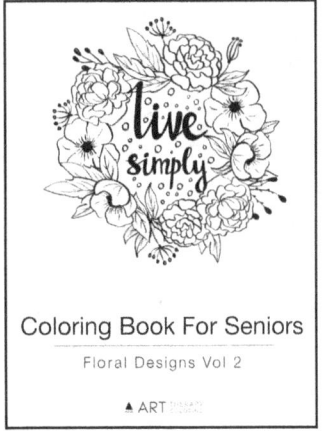

live simply
Coloring Book For Seniors
Floral Designs Vol 2

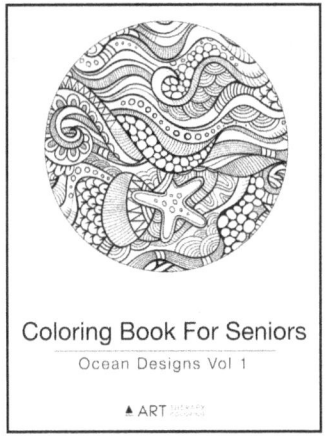

Coloring Book For Seniors
Ocean Designs Vol 1

Coloring Books For Teens

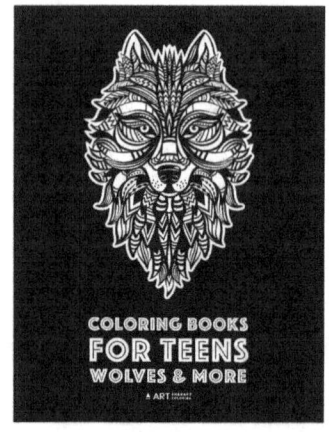

COLORING BOOKS FOR TEENS WOLVES & MORE

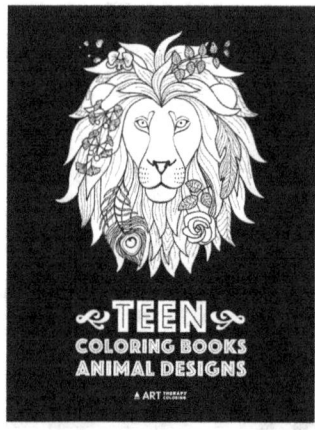

~TEEN~ COLORING BOOKS ANIMAL DESIGNS

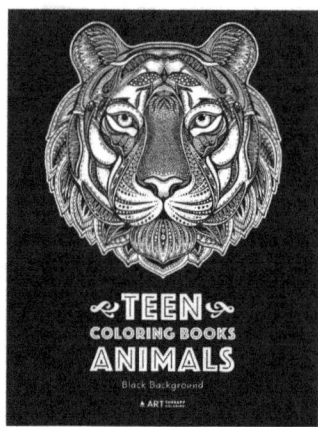

~TEEN~ COLORING BOOKS ANIMALS
Black Background

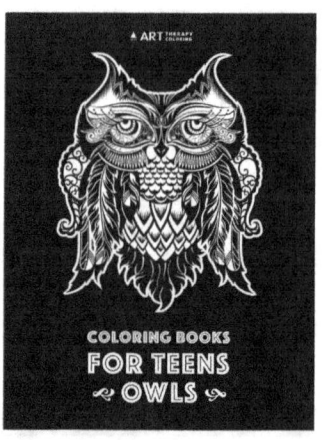

COLORING BOOKS FOR TEENS ~OWLS~

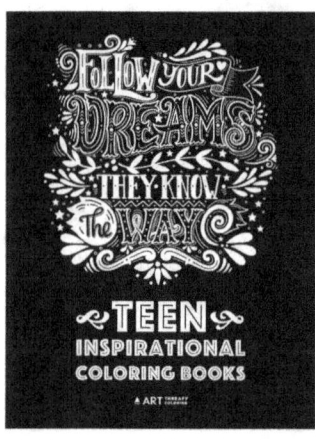

~TEEN~ INSPIRATIONAL COLORING BOOKS

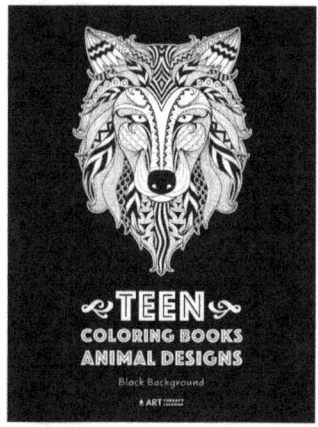

~TEEN~ COLORING BOOKS ANIMAL DESIGNS
Black Background

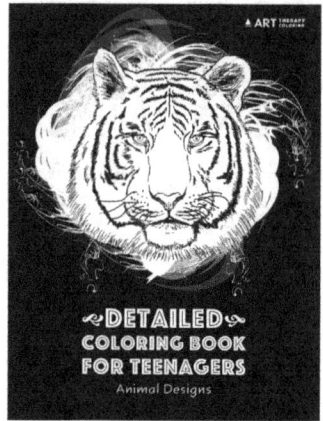

~DETAILED~ COLORING BOOK FOR TEENAGERS
Animal Designs

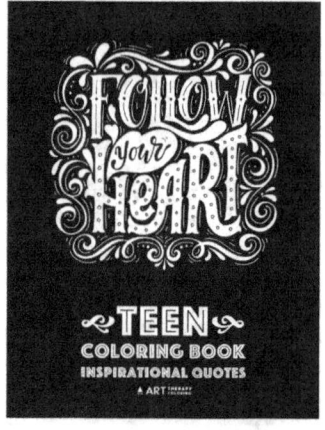

~TEEN~ COLORING BOOK INSPIRATIONAL QUOTES

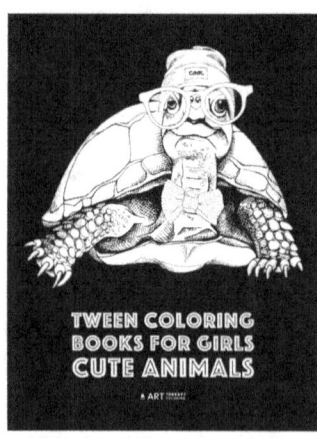

TWEEN COLORING BOOKS FOR GIRLS CUTE ANIMALS

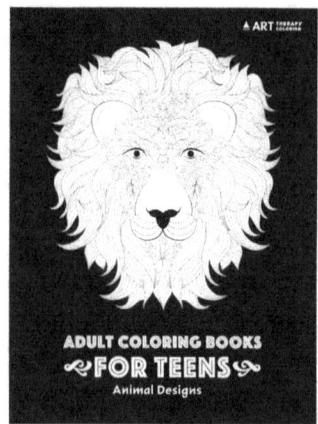

ADULT COLORING BOOKS ~FOR TEENS~
Animal Designs

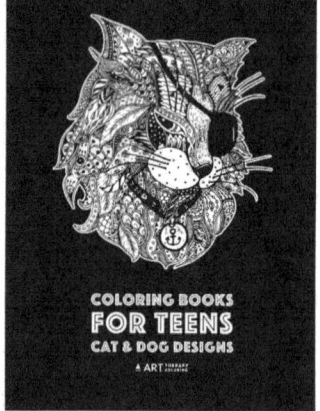

COLORING BOOKS FOR TEENS CAT & DOG DESIGNS

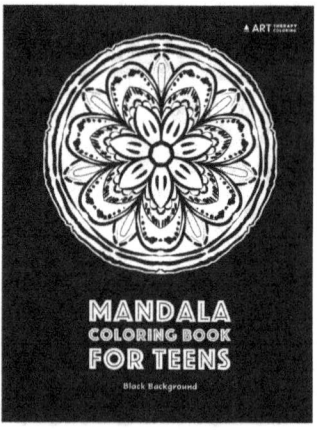

MANDALA COLORING BOOK FOR TEENS
Black Background

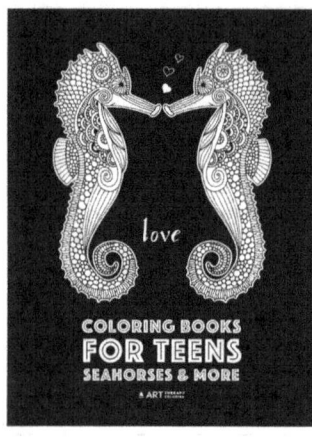

COLORING BOOKS FOR TEENS SEAHORSES & MORE

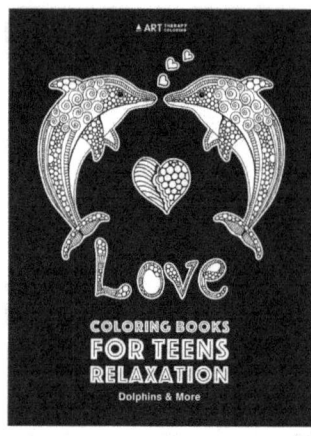

COLORING BOOKS FOR TEENS RELAXATION
Dolphins & More

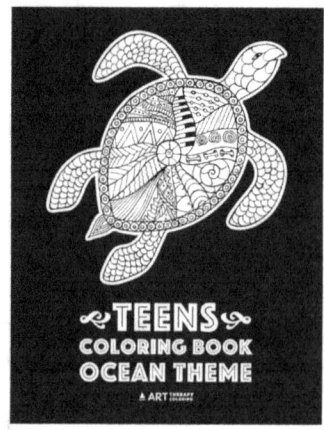

~TEENS~ COLORING BOOK OCEAN THEME

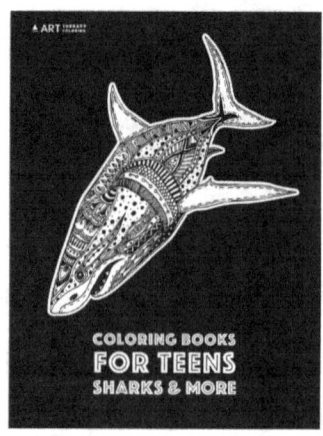

COLORING BOOKS FOR TEENS SHARKS & MORE

Coloring Books For Teens

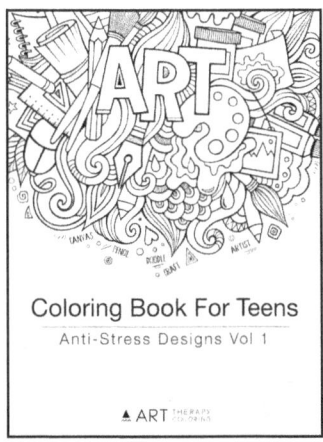

Coloring Book For Teens

Anti-Stress Designs Vol 1

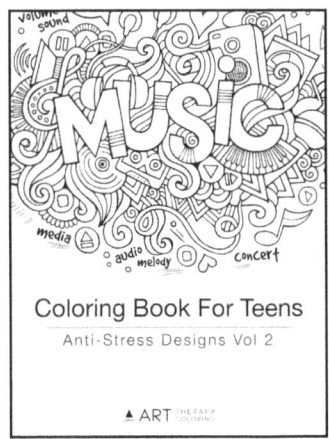

Coloring Book For Teens

Anti-Stress Designs Vol 2

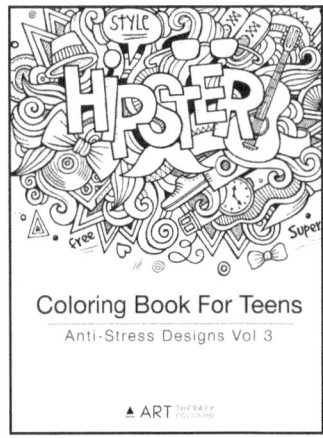

Coloring Book For Teens

Anti-Stress Designs Vol 3

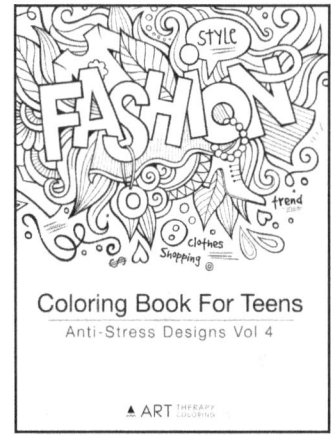

Coloring Book For Teens

Anti-Stress Designs Vol 4

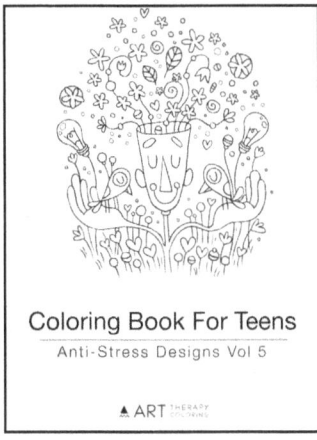

Coloring Book For Teens

Anti-Stress Designs Vol 5

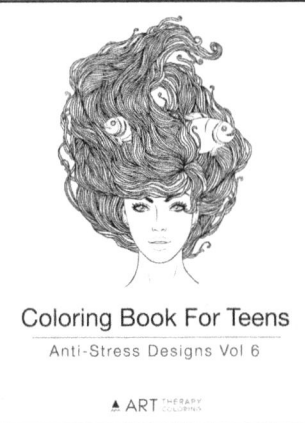

Coloring Book For Teens

Anti-Stress Designs Vol 6

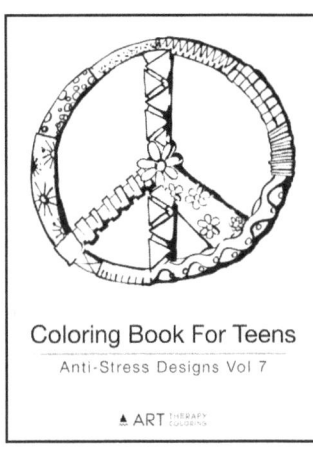

Coloring Book For Teens

Anti-Stress Designs Vol 7

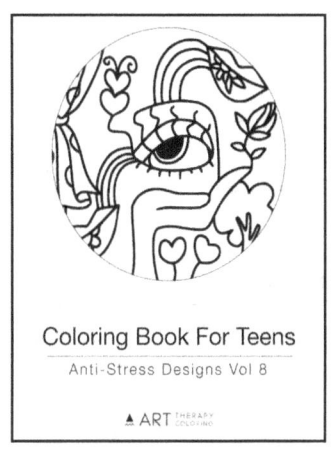

Coloring Book For Teens

Anti-Stress Designs Vol 8

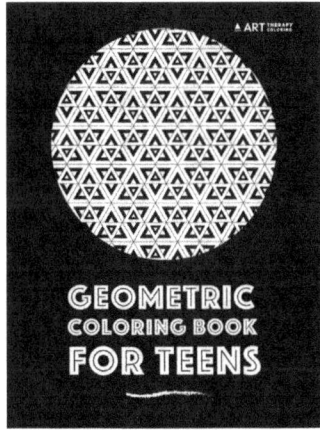

GEOMETRIC COLORING BOOK FOR TEENS

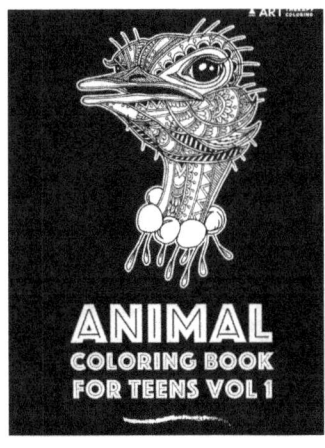

ANIMAL COLORING BOOK FOR TEENS VOL 1

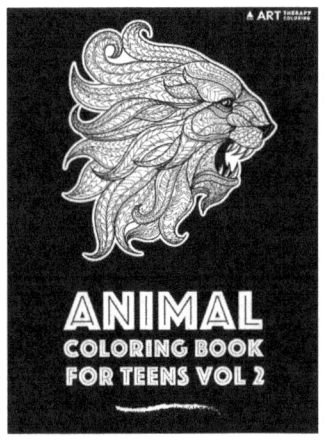

ANIMAL COLORING BOOK FOR TEENS VOL 2

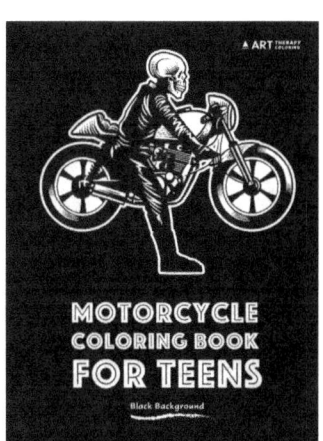

MOTORCYCLE COLORING BOOK FOR TEENS
Black Background

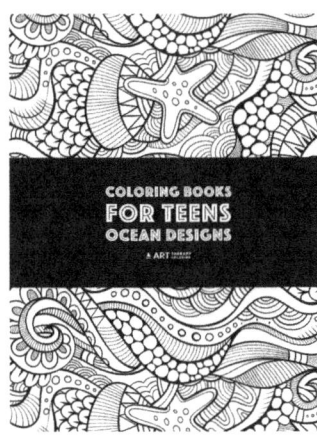

COLORING BOOKS FOR TEENS OCEAN DESIGNS

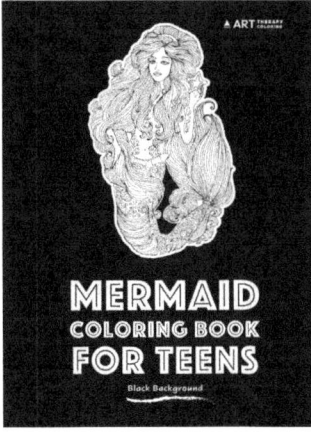

MERMAID COLORING BOOK FOR TEENS
Black Background

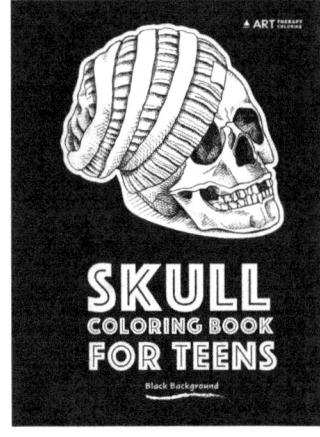

SKULL COLORING BOOK FOR TEENS
Black Background

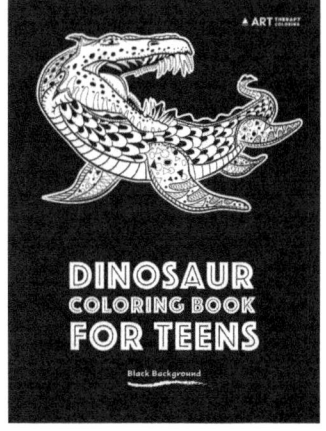

DINOSAUR COLORING BOOK FOR TEENS
Black Background

Coloring Books For Girls

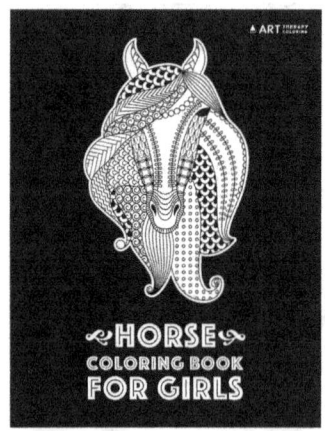

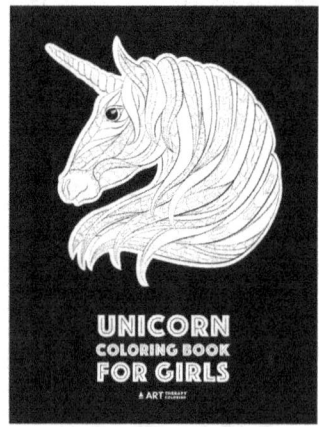

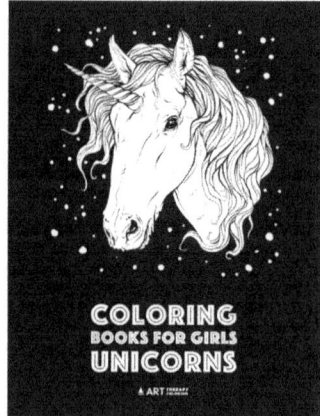

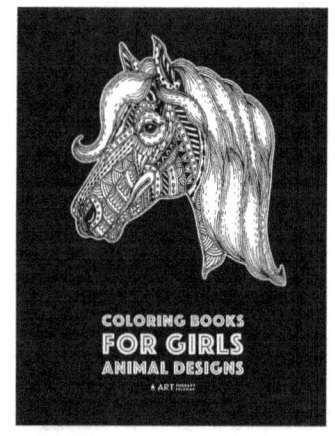

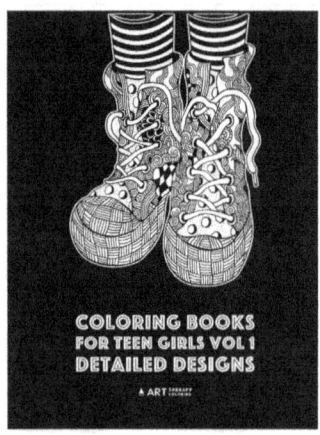

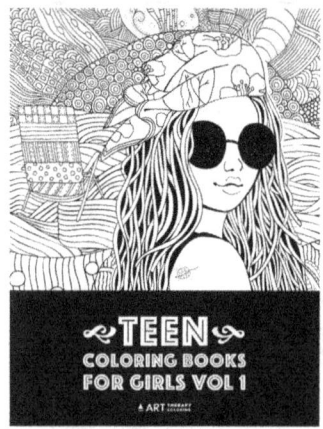

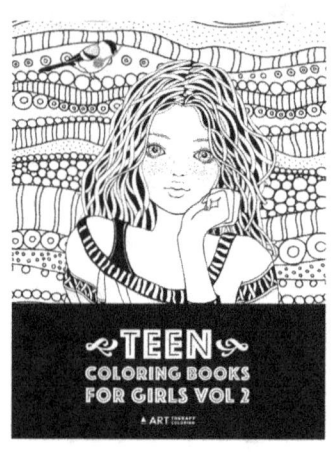

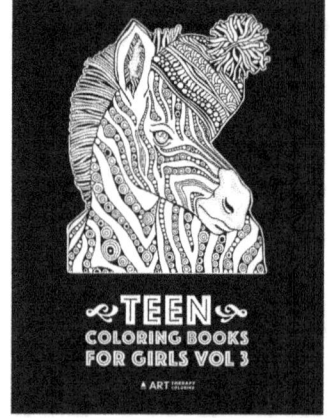

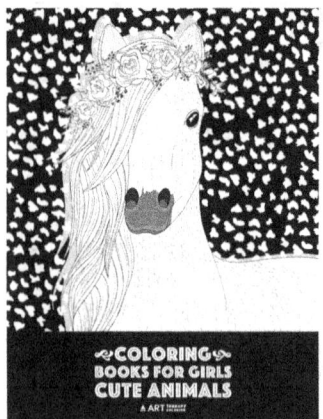

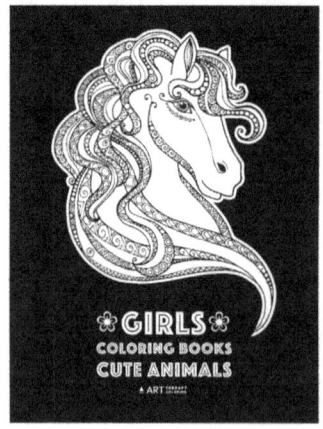

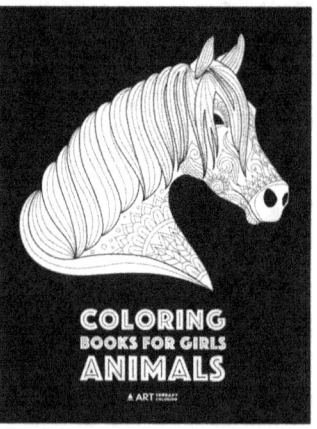

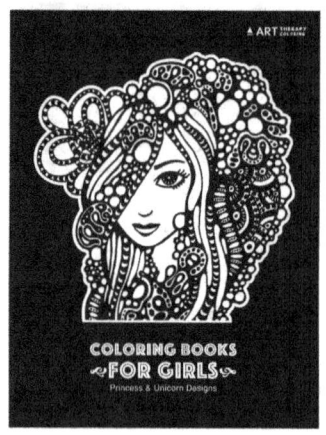

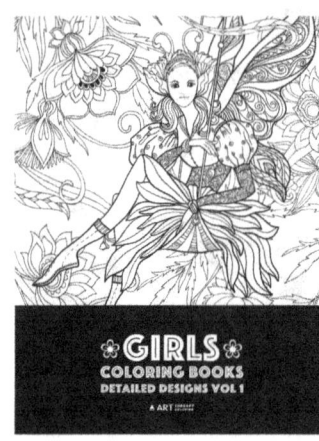

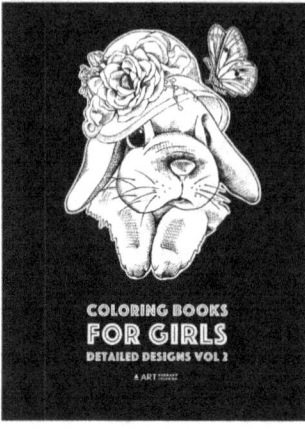

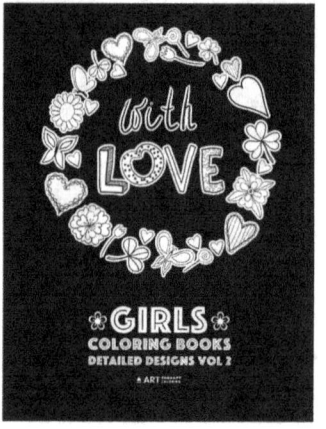

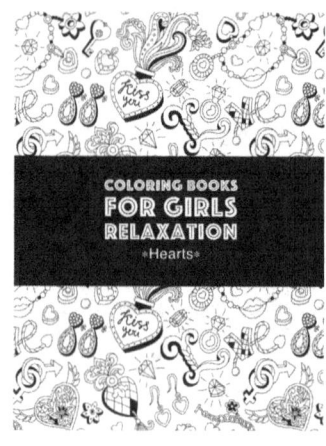

Art Therapy Coloring Books

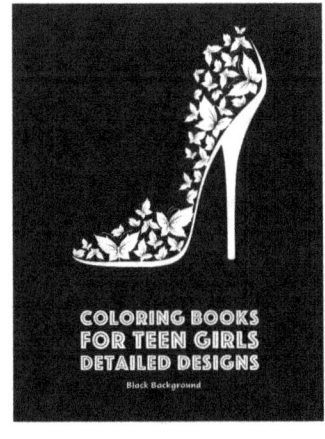

COLORING BOOKS FOR TEEN GIRLS DETAILED DESIGNS
Black Background

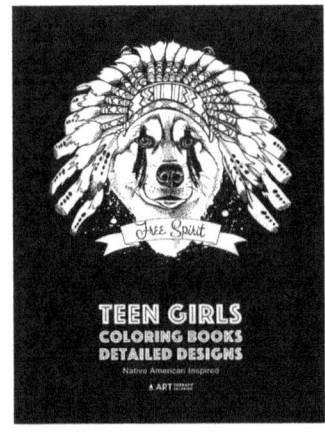

TEEN GIRLS COLORING BOOKS DETAILED DESIGNS
Native American Inspired

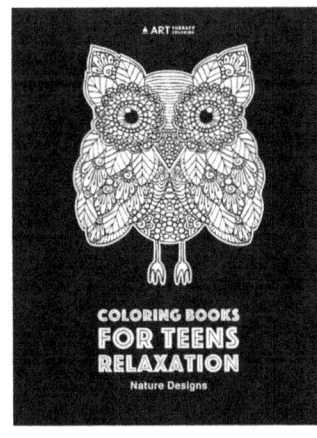

COLORING BOOKS FOR TEENS RELAXATION
Nature Designs

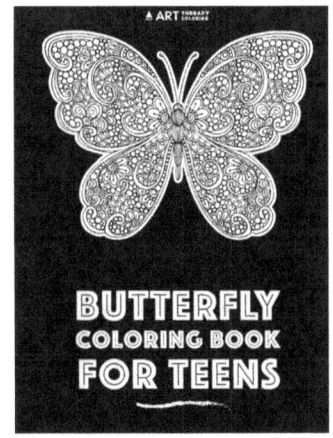

BUTTERFLY COLORING BOOK FOR TEENS

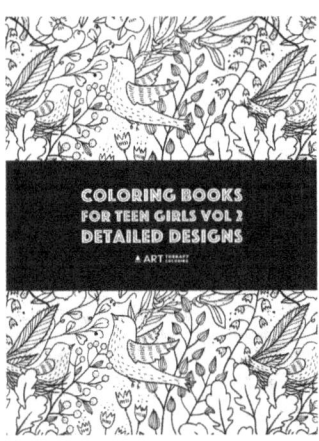

COLORING BOOKS FOR TEEN GIRLS VOL 2 DETAILED DESIGNS

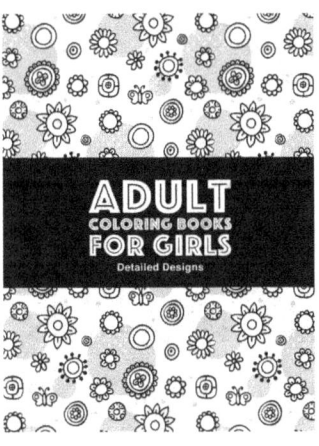

ADULT COLORING BOOKS FOR GIRLS
Detailed Designs

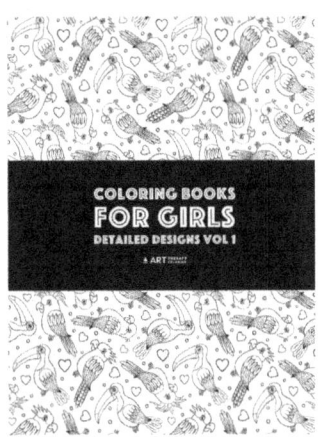

COLORING BOOKS FOR GIRLS DETAILED DESIGNS VOL 1

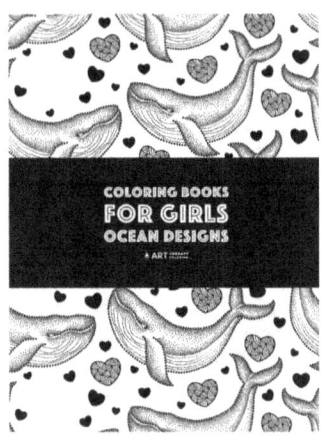

COLORING BOOKS FOR GIRLS OCEAN DESIGNS

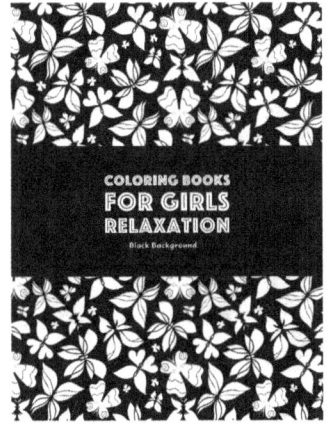

COLORING BOOKS FOR GIRLS RELAXATION
Black Background

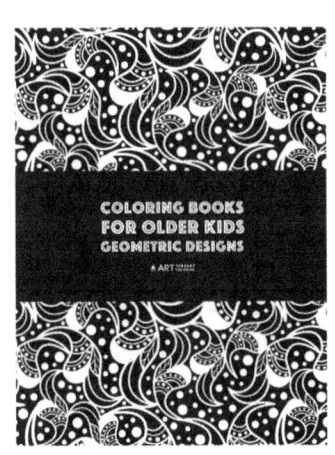

COLORING BOOKS FOR OLDER KIDS GEOMETRIC DESIGNS

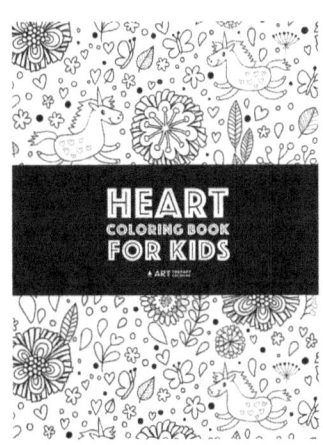

HEART COLORING BOOK FOR KIDS

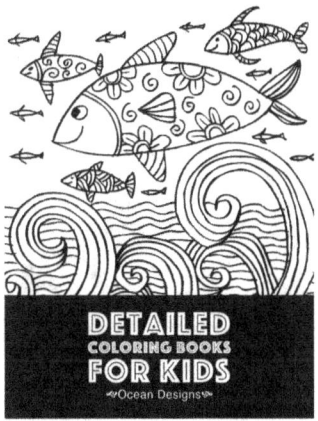

DETAILED COLORING BOOK FOR KIDS
Ocean Designs

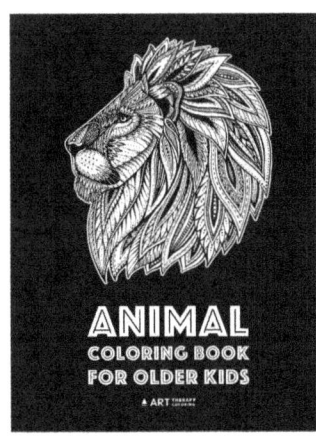

ANIMAL COLORING BOOK FOR OLDER KIDS

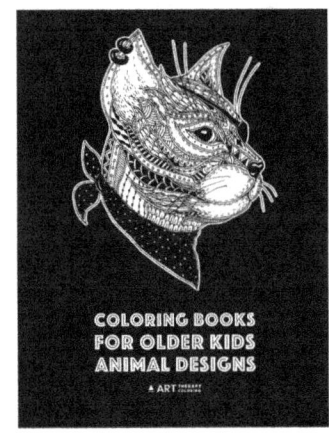

COLORING BOOKS FOR OLDER KIDS ANIMAL DESIGNS

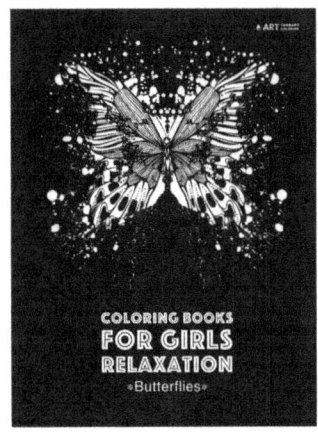

COLORING BOOKS FOR GIRLS RELAXATION
Butterflies

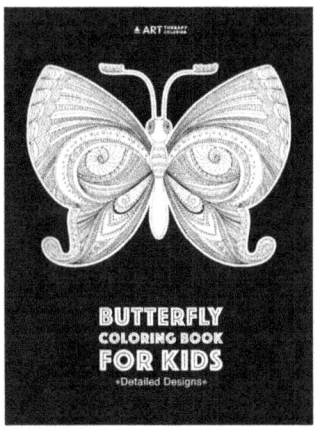

BUTTERFLY COLORING BOOK FOR KIDS
Detailed Designs

Coloring Books For Boys

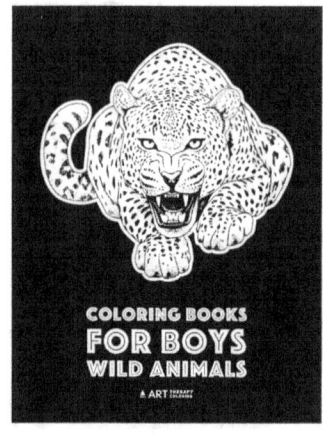

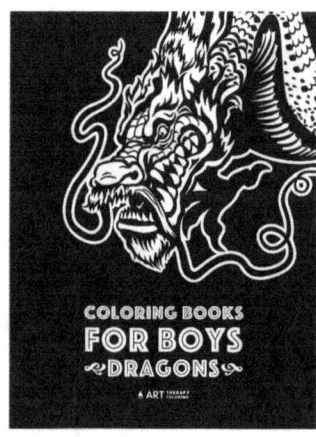

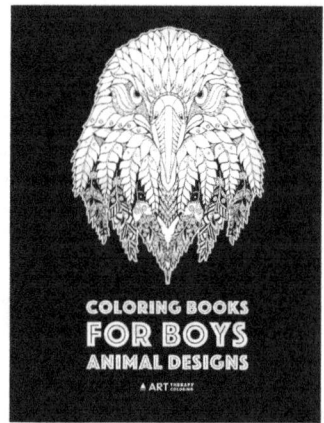

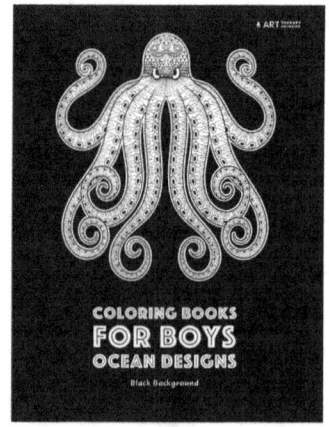

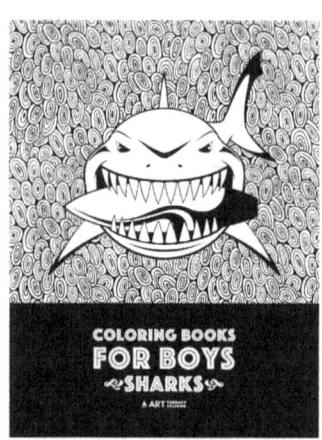

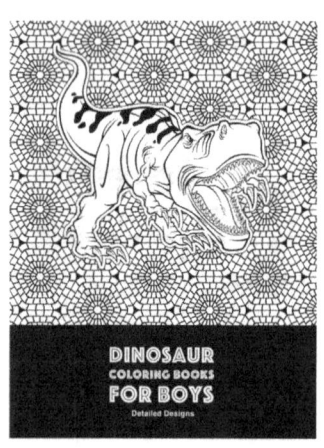

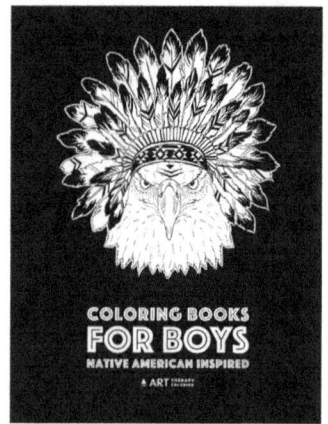

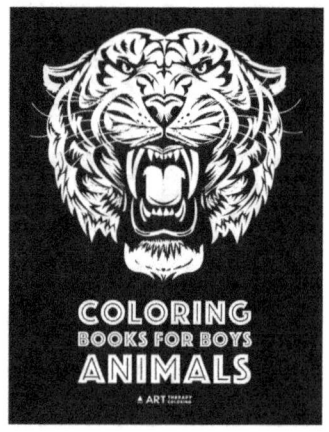

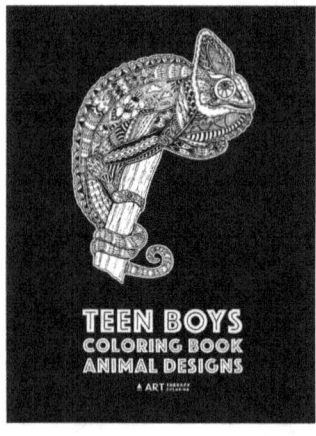

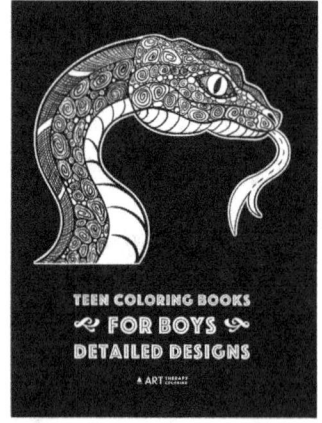

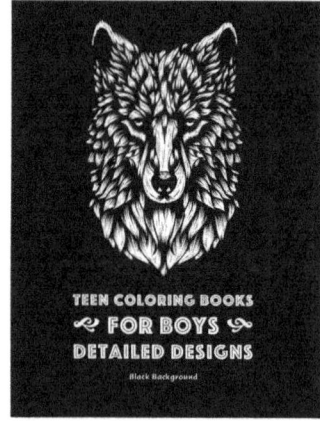

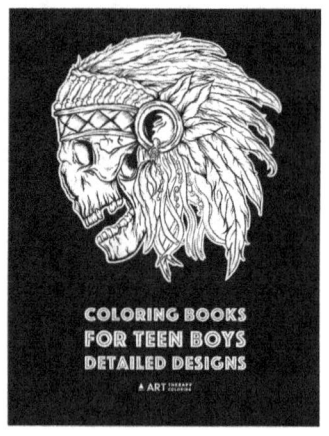

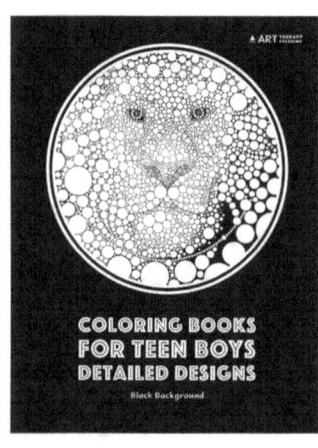

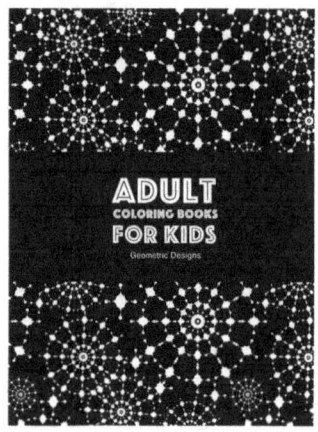

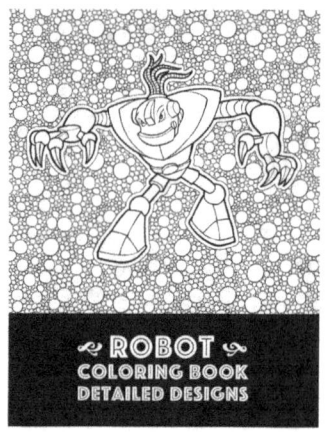

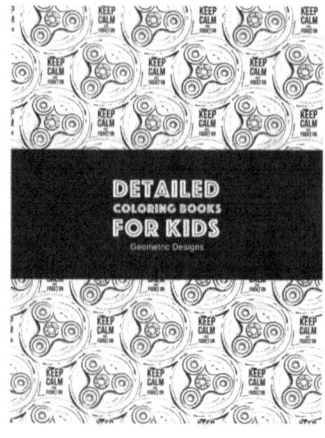

Coloring Books For Kids

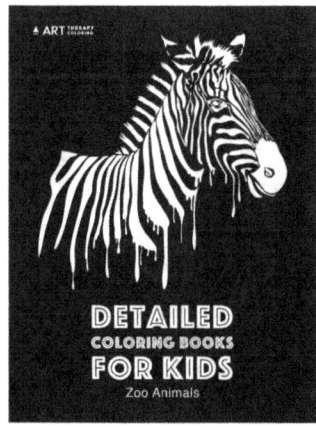

DETAILED
COLORING BOOKS
FOR KIDS
Zoo Animals

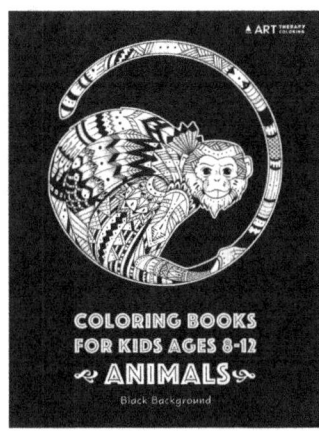

COLORING BOOKS
FOR KIDS AGES 8-12
ANIMALS
Black Background

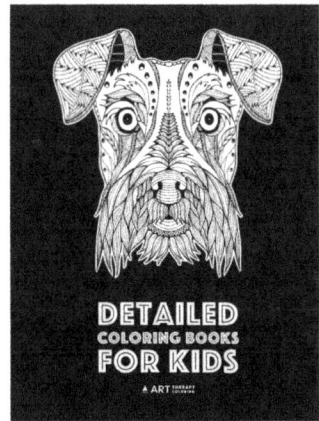

DETAILED
COLORING BOOKS
FOR KIDS

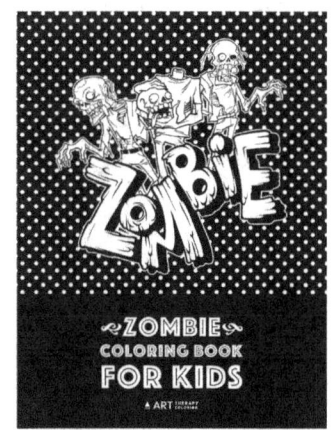

ZOMBIE
COLORING BOOK
FOR KIDS

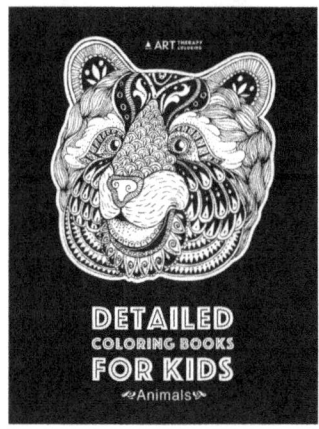

DETAILED
COLORING BOOKS
FOR KIDS
Animals

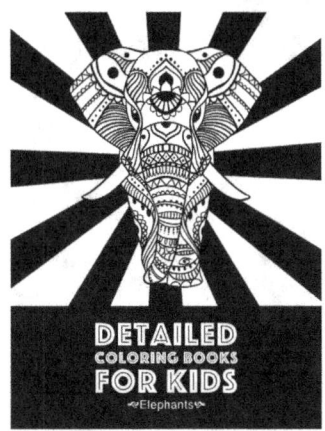

DETAILED
COLORING BOOKS
FOR KIDS
Elephants

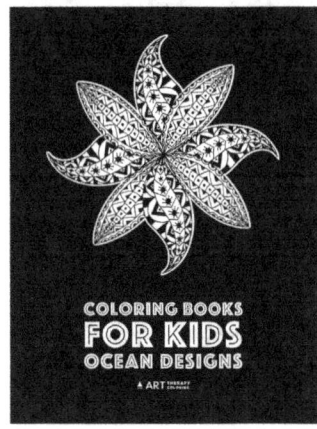

COLORING BOOKS
FOR KIDS
OCEAN DESIGNS

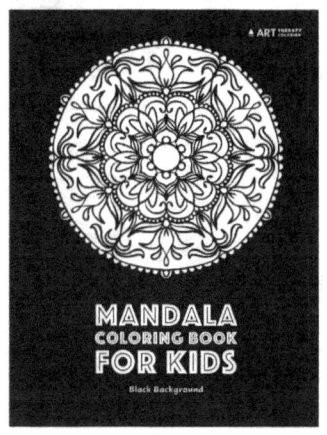

MANDALA
COLORING BOOK
FOR KIDS
Black Background

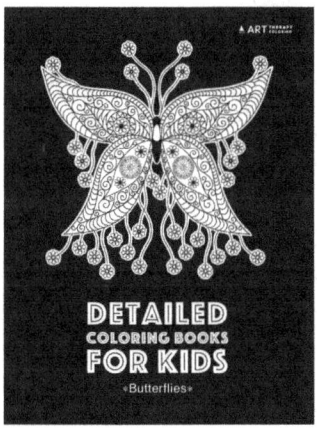

DETAILED
COLORING BOOKS
FOR KIDS
Butterflies

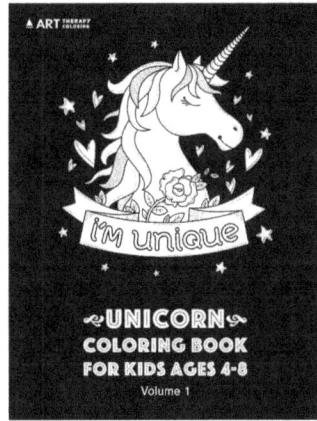

UNICORN
COLORING BOOK
FOR KIDS AGES 4-8
Volume 1

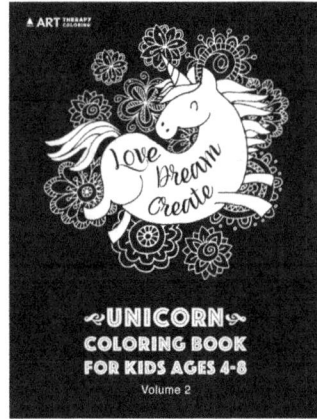

UNICORN
COLORING BOOK
FOR KIDS AGES 4-8
Volume 2

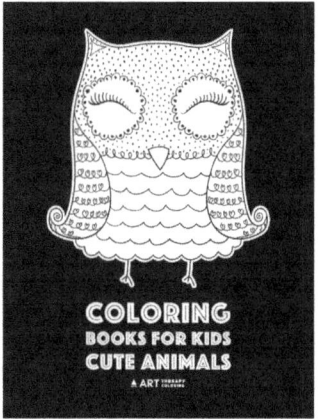

COLORING
BOOKS FOR KIDS
CUTE ANIMALS

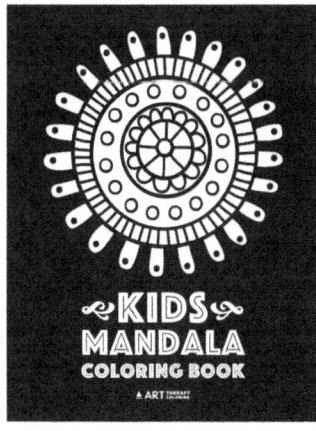

KIDS
MANDALA
COLORING BOOK

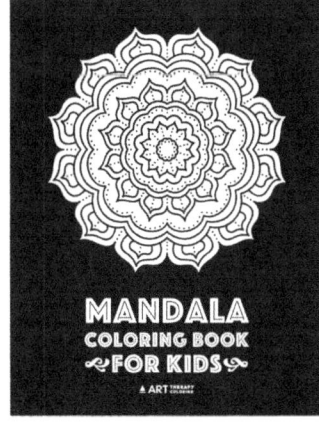

MANDALA
COLORING BOOK
FOR KIDS

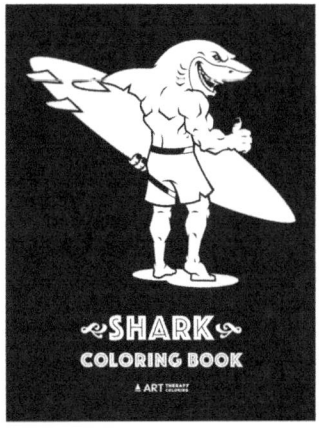

SHARK
COLORING BOOK

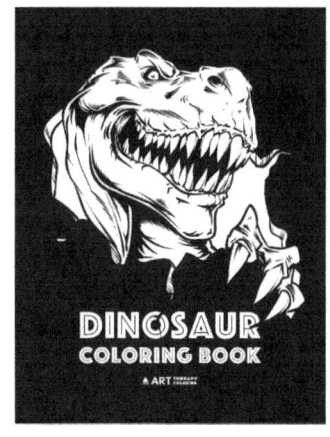

DINOSAUR
COLORING BOOK

Coloring Books For Special Occasions

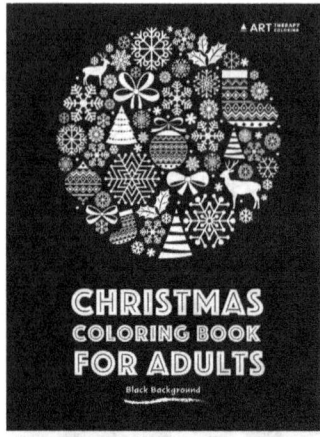
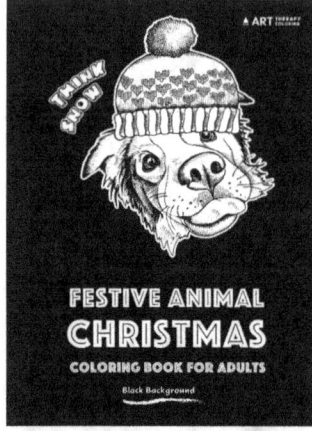
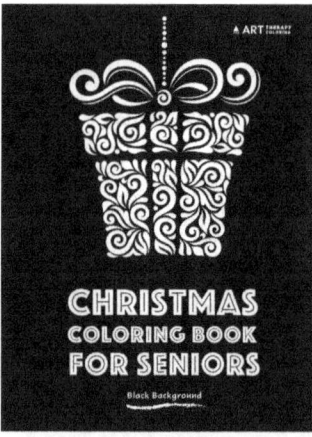
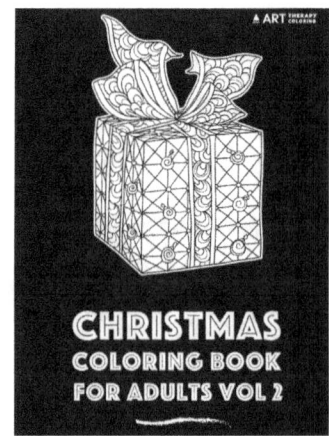

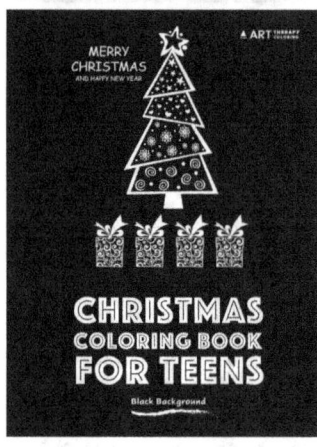
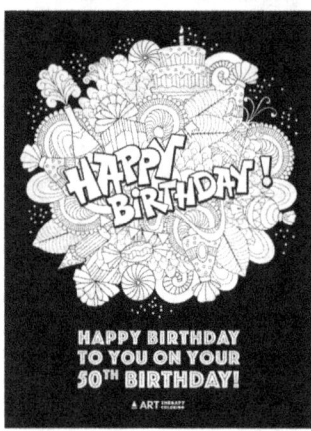
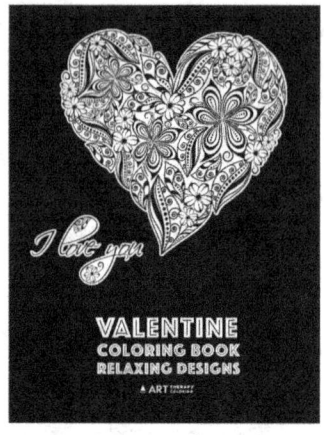
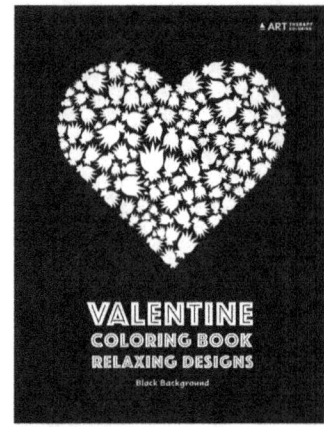

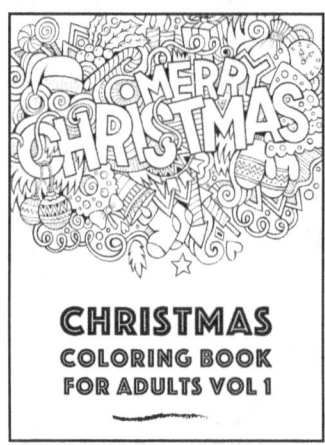
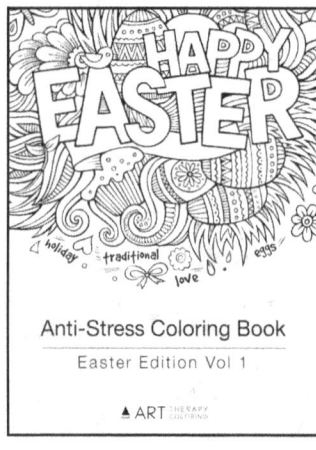
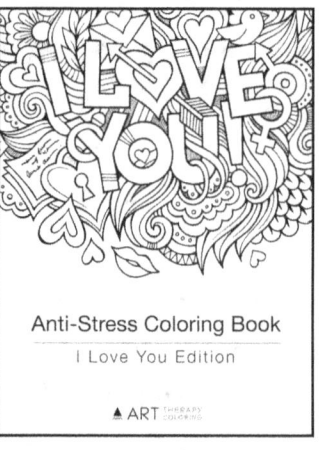
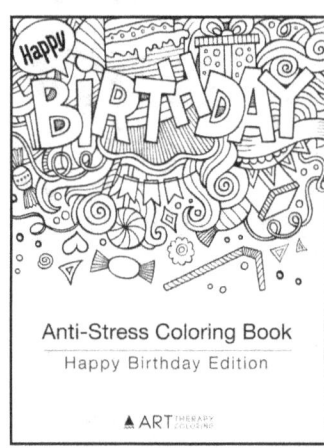

Valentine Coloring Book
Relaxing Designs

Published by:
Art Therapy Coloring
El Dorado Hills, California
www.arttherapycoloring.com

Shutterstock Images

ISBN: 978-1-64126-025-1